CONFIDENT PLURALISM

CONFIDENT PLURALISM

SURVIVING AND THRIVING

THROUGH DEEP DIFFERENCE

JOHN D. INAZU

THE UNIVERSITY OF CHICAGO PRESS

Chicago and London

John D. Inazu *is associate professor of law and political science at Washington University in St. Louis.*

The University of Chicago Press, Chicago 60637
The University of Chicago Press, Ltd., London
© 2016 by The University of Chicago
All rights reserved. Published 2016.
Printed in the United States of America

25 24 23 22 21 20 19 18 17   7 8 9 10 11 12

ISBN-13: 978-0-226-36545-9 (cloth)
ISBN-13: 978-0-226-36559-6 (e-book)
DOI: 10.7208/chicago/9780226365596.001.0001

Library of Congress Cataloguing-in-Publication Data

Inazu, John D., author.
    Confident pluralism : surviving and thriving through deep
    difference / John D. Inazu.
        pages   cm
    Includes bibliographical references and index.
    ISBN 978-0-226-36545-9 (cloth : alkaline paper)
    ISBN 978-0-226-36559-6 (e-book)
    1. Multiculturalism—United States. 2. Cultural pluralism—
    United States. 3. Constitutional law—Social aspects—United
    States. I. Title.
    HN90.M84153 2016
    305.800973—dc23

                                                     2015035279

♾ This paper meets the requirements of ANSI/NISO Z39.48-1992
(Permanence of Paper).

For Lauren, Hana, and Sam

contents

INTRODUCTION

It was just a thought experiment.

My law and religion class had turned to the relationship between school funding and the First Amendment's prohibition on the establishment of religion. The big question in this area of the law is where to draw the line between "appropriate" and "inappropriate" government funding of religious schools. The key case is a 1947 Supreme Court decision about whether taxpayer dollars could reimburse parents for the cost of bus fares to transport their children to Catholic schools. The intellectual puzzle has confounded courts for decades: if tax dollars can pay for buses, then what about textbooks, prayer books, and Bibles? Conversely, if they can't pay for buses, then what about public roads and crossing guards near the schools?[1]

Law professors make a living out of posing hypotheticals, and I threw one out to the class. The Catholic Church, as most people know, restricts its priestly office to men. That position puts it at odds with some contemporary norms about gender equality. Suppose that a city government provided crossing guards to all of its public and private schools because it had good evidence that fewer schoolchildren would be hurt or killed with those guards in place. The guards cost taxpayer dollars. Could the city refuse to pay for guards at the Catholic school because of the school's views about gender?

I had expected some back-and-forth, but I was surprised when one student dug in: "Yes, absolutely. The school has chosen to place itself outside of the acceptable bounds of society—it is not entitled to any services of the state. The state need not 'subsidize' such institutions." I pressed further: "What if the school catches on fire? Can the fire department refuse to answer the call?" "Yes," the student responded. "The school has made a choice. It can try to put out the fire on its own." "Well," I asked, "what if there is an active shooter in the school? Should the SWAT team just stand by and wait for the shooter to finish up?" The student replied, "I don't see why not."

To be sure, it was just a classroom hypothetical. There was also a certain logic to my student's responses: if we're serious about disentangling government from any "support" or "subsidizing" of anti-orthodox positions, then maybe we should go all the way. And even if most of us would not go that far, plenty of people call for the marginalization of their neighbors in other ways. Some of us make comments that push in the direction of my student's answers: we may not want to see schools burning or SWAT teams standing down, but we would just as soon see those with whom we disagree shut up, move away, or disappear.

These kinds of views are especially prominent in political commentary. Conservative newsman Bill O'Reilly says that professional athletes who join protests about racial injustice "[aren't] smart enough to know what they're doing." Theater critic Michael Feingold suggests that Republicans "should be exterminated before they cause any more harm." Talk show host Rush Limbaugh calls law student Sandra Fluke a "slut" because she supported contraception coverage under the Affordable Care Act. *Slate* editor J. Bryan Lowder writes that "it would be enough for me if those people who are so ignorant or intransigent as to still be anti-gay in 2014 would simply shut up." Former Obama speechwriter Jon Lovett has dubbed our political discourse "the culture of shut up."[2]

Our antipathy for the viewpoints and values of others extends beyond words. Consider the following examples:

- In 2012 North Carolina voters passed an amendment that constitutionalized the state's definition of marriage between a man and a woman and invalidated other forms of "domestic legal union." The amendment potentially jeopardized protections for gays and lesbians in family law, domestic violence law, estate planning, and employee benefits.[3]

- Across the state of California today, many conservative religious student groups are no longer welcome on the campuses of many public colleges and universities. And it's not just a West Coast thing. Vanderbilt University, Bowdoin College, and a number of other schools have also kicked out conservative religious groups. These schools rely on "all-comers" policies that require student groups to admit as members—and even leaders—any student who wishes to participate. The Republican club must accept Democrats. The pro-choice club must accept pro-lifers. Conservative religious groups with membership or leadership restrictions are unable to comply. These policies send a clear message to conservative religious groups: change or leave.[4]

- In November 2014 Alabama voters passed a constitutional amendment prohibiting state courts from applying foreign law that would violate state or federal law. The amendment— the result of much fear-mongering about the incursions of Sharia law—had no legal consequences; it was, as University of Alabama law professor Paul Horwitz noted, "completely redundant" in light of existing laws. But it was not without symbolic effect, and traded on anti-Muslim hostility to draw voters to the ballot box. Over thirty states have considered similar amendments or legislation.[5]

Here's another example, with less overt hostility but deep tensions just below the surface. Wellesley College, an all-women's school, now confronts internal challenges around its growing transgender student population. Even though Wellesley admits only women, a number of its current students have transitioned to men after matriculation. As a recent *New York Times* story asks: "What's a women's college to do? Trans students point out that they're doing exactly what these schools encourage: breaking gender barriers,

fulfilling their deepest yearnings and forging ahead even when society tries to hold them back. But yielding to their request to dilute
the focus on women would undercut the identity of a women's college." One student reasoned: "I realized that if we excluded trans
students, we'd be fighting on the wrong team. We'd be on the wrong
side of history." A recent graduate reached the opposite conclusion:
"Sisterhood is why I chose to go to Wellesley." The *New York Times*
noted that this woman "asked not to be identified for fear she'd be
denounced for her opinion."[6]

This last example exposes a particularly acute challenge: Wellesley cannot remain a women's college whose identity in some ways
rests on gender exclusivity and at the same time welcome transgender students who identify as men. It will have to choose between two competing views. But perhaps even more important
than *what* decision Wellesley reaches is *how* it reaches that decision. Will Wellesley be able to choose its own institutional identity, or will the government impose a norm on the private school
through law and regulation? Will other citizens tolerate Wellesley's
choice, or will they challenge its accreditation, boycott its events,
and otherwise malign its existence? Will the process through which
Wellesley reaches its decision be one of open engagement across
deep difference, or will students, faculty, and administrators speak
only under the cover of anonymity?

OUR DEEP DIFFERENCES

The examples that I've recounted point to some of our differences
over questions of politics, religion, and sexuality. We could all name
many other issues that divide us. These deep and often irresolvable differences call into question our constitutional aspiration for
"a more perfect union," our national metaphor of a great "melting
pot," and the promise of our nation's seal, *E pluribus unum* ("Out
of many, one").

Our differences pervade our beliefs, preferences, and allegiances.
They affect not only what we think, but also *how* we think, and how
we see the world. The philosopher John Rawls called it the "fact of
pluralism"—the recognition that we live in a society of "a plurality

of conflicting, and indeed incommensurable, conceptions of the meaning, value and purpose of human life."[7]

Not all of our differences are problematic. Most of us think some difference is good, that this variety of perspective makes life more interesting. I think the world is a better place because I pull for the Duke Blue Devils and some of my friends cheer for lesser basketball teams. March Madness would be less interesting if everybody liked Duke and nobody cheered against them. We might reach a similar conclusion about beauty, taste, and humor. Some of these differences enrich our lives. Some of them lead to sharper thinking and greater creativity.[8]

On the other hand, most of us do not think that all difference is good. We can all name things that we think the world would be better off without. This is especially true when it comes to our moral beliefs. We might prefer a society in which everyone agreed about what counts as a justifiable homicide, a mean temperament, or a good life.

To complicate matters, we also disagree over the nature of our disagreements, and over how much disagreement is a good thing. Moreover, at least some of our most important beliefs cannot be reconciled with one another. It cannot be the case that the act of abortion is both morally acceptable and morally intolerable. It cannot be the case that God exists and that God does not exist. And these differences matter far more than basketball allegiances. What are we to do in light of our deeply held disagreements?

The French philosopher Jean-Jacques Rousseau offered one response: "it is impossible to live at peace with those we regard as damned." We see echoes of Rousseau's bleak pronouncement in recent skirmishes between conservative religious beliefs and gay rights. Consider the ferocious debate that erupted over an Indiana religious liberty law in March 2015. Conservative radio host Mark Levin contended that opponents of the law "hate America." Family Research Council president Tony Perkins argued that any changes to the law "would gut religious freedom in Indiana." In the other direction, Apple CEO Tim Cook was just as hyperbolic, calling the law a "very dangerous" effort to "enshrine discrimination" and "rationalize injustice." And journalist Ben Kepes worried that the law "feels very much like a prelude to another Kristallnacht." Meanwhile, the actual legal debate focused on whether a few Christian florists and cake bakers (and, apparently, one hapless pizza joint) could refuse to provide their services for a same-sex wedding. That question is not trivial, and had powerful symbolic meaning for both sides. But the policy implications did not merit the overheated rhetoric or portend the kind of consequences the rhetoric suggested.[9]

Other parts of the world experience far worse than irresponsible rhetoric. Rousseau's prediction has played out more concretely in places like Rwanda, Somalia, South Africa, and the Middle East. As author Shadi Hamid has argued, we cannot dismiss the developments in Gaza, Syria, and Iraq as rooted in "ancient hatreds." Rather, the deterioration in the Middle East results from a "collective loss of faith in politics." We see even more striking examples of Rousseau's claim in the slaughter of innocents by groups like Al Qaeda and ISIS. The impossibility of living in peace with those we think are damned ultimately leads to what Hamid calls "the end of pluralism."[10]

The end of pluralism is a nightmare.

Confident Pluralism insists that Rousseau was wrong: our shared existence is not only possible, but also necessary. Confident pluralism offers a political solution to the practical problem of our deep differences. Instead of the elusive goal of *E pluribus unum*, it suggests a more modest possibility—that we can live together in our "many-ness." That vision does not entail Pollyannaish illusions that we will overcome our differences and live happily ever after. We will continue to struggle with those whose views we regard as irrational, immoral, or even dangerous. We are stuck with the good, the bad, and the ugly of pluralism. Yet confident pluralism remains possible in both law and society.

Confident pluralism takes both *confidence* and *pluralism* seriously. Confidence without pluralism misses the reality of politics. It suppresses difference, sometimes violently. Pluralism without confidence misses the reality of people. It ignores or trivializes our stark differences for the sake of feigned agreement and false unity. Confident pluralism allows genuine difference to coexist without suppressing or minimizing our firmly held convictions. We can embrace pluralism precisely because we are confident in our own beliefs, and in the groups and institutions that sustain them.

This confidence in our own convictions reinforces our differences and increases the risk of friction. For this reason, confident pluralism differs from a number of other proposals that seek consensus across difference, including various strands of Rawlsian liberalism and, before that, mid-twentieth-century liberalism. It comes much closer to law professor Abner Greene's claim that consensus proposals seek a "false solace" in attempting to overcome difference and "we do better by recognizing difference as something we can't get past." Confident pluralism does not suppress or ignore conflict—it invites it.[11]

At the same time, confident pluralism recognizes that we have better and worse ways to live out our own confidence and to negotiate the pluralism around us. Confident pluralism should not be misread as the rejection of any consensus at all—it is not an invitation to anarchy. Like any serious proposal of how to live together in society, it draws upon certain shared resources and common aspirations. We retain some modest unity in our diversity.[12]

The origins of the phrase "confident pluralism" point toward these possibilities. In 2010 the United States Supreme Court upheld the validity of an "all-comers" policy at a public law school in San Francisco. That decision, *Christian Legal Society v. Martinez*, rejected the First Amendment claims of a Christian group that required members to be celibate outside of heterosexual marriage. The case triggered a wave of similar policies that have removed conservative religious groups from college campuses. During the litigation, the group Gays and Lesbians for Individual Liberty (GLIL) filed a brief highlighting some of the problems with the "all-comers" policy. Founded in 1991, GLIL promotes "tolerance and acceptance of homosexuals among members of the wider society." It strongly disagreed with the membership policies of the Christian group. But it argued that the "all-comers" policy unwisely sacrificed associational freedom. The brief concluded that "the First Amendment envisions a better way: A *confident pluralism* that conduces to civil peace and advances democratic consensus-building."[13]

The goal of confident pluralism is not to settle which views are right and which views are wrong. Rather, it proposes that the future of our democratic experiment requires finding a way to be steadfast in our personal convictions, while also making room for the cacophony that may ensue when others disagree with us. Confident pluralism allows us to function—and even to flourish—despite the divisions arising out of our deeply held beliefs. These observations are consistent with Harvard Law dean Martha Minow's assertion that "whether through a principled commitment to tolerate others or a pragmatic commitment to survive, we who live in plural worlds must exhibit enough mutual respect at least to coexist."[14]

This book is an argument for mutual respect and coexistence. It is built on the twofold premise that confident pluralism remains possible in both law and society. We can think of these possibilities in terms of constitutional commitments and civic practices, respectively. The first part of the book (chapters 1–4) sets out the constitutional commitments. The second part of the book (chapters 5–8) turns to the civic practices.

CONSTITUTIONAL COMMITMENTS

Chapters 1–4 contend that recent constitutional doctrine has departed from our longstanding embrace of pluralism and the political arrangements that make pluralism possible. The arguments in these first four chapters are meant to engage scholars, judges, and policymakers who have undervalued and weakened protections for the voluntary groups of civil society, the public forum, and certain forms of generally available funding. They are also meant to educate citizens about the poor state of the current legal doctrine in these areas, and to encourage political solutions where judicial ones have failed.

Chapter 1 begins with the modest unity that allows us to coexist in political community rather than in anarchy. One reason that confident pluralism is possible is that we retain some minimal agreement about our society even in the midst of our deep differences. Part of this agreement recognizes the wisdom of individual rights that guard against state-enforced orthodoxy and allow us to create meaning apart from majoritarian norms. Our modest unity also includes two premises, inclusion and dissent. The inclusion premise is that we seek for those within our boundaries to be part of the political community. The dissent premise is that we allow for people to dissent from the norms established by that community.

Chapter 2 sets out the cornerstone of confident pluralism's constitutional commitments: the protections for individuals to form and gather in groups of their choosing. These protections are under pressure from modern changes to the right of association focusing on intimacy and expressiveness. Intimate association protects very few actual groups. Expressive association, which emerges most clearly in two Supreme Court decisions—*Roberts v. United States Jaycees* and *Boy Scouts of America v. Dale*—lacks a coherent framework and leaves certain groups deemed "nonexpressive" particularly vulnerable. Chapter 2 explores these ideas through the Top Hatters Motorcycle Club and the Muslim Student Association. It explores the importance of strengthening protections for the voluntary groups of civil society. Let's call this the "voluntary groups requirement."

Chapter 3 introduces the related concept of the public forum through the popular television show *Parks & Recreation*. Real-life public forums, like the forums depicted in *Parks & Recreation*, are government-provided spaces where viewpoints become voices. They are an essential part of confident pluralism because they allow citizens and the groups that they form to advocate, protest, and witness in common spaces—and they are insufficiently protected under current constitutional doctrine. We have seen these weaknesses exposed in a variety of settings, including the crackdown on protests in Ferguson, Missouri, restrictions against labor activism, and regulation of anti-abortion protesters. A separate challenge arises because public forums are not the only places where we enact the aspirations of confident pluralism—privately owned spaces like coffee shops, parks, and online service providers increasingly serve this function. Ordinary citizens need either spaces provided and facilitated by the government or "private public forums" to come together for purposes of dissent, disagreement, and diversity. Let's call this the "public forum requirement."

Chapter 4 shows how some forms of government funding are indispensable to the vision of confident pluralism. Using as a case study the 1970s magazine *Big Mama Rag*, chapter 4 explains why the government's discretion with its money—or rather, with our money—is not unlimited. Confident pluralism argues that when government actors create and maintain generally available funding that facilitates a diversity of viewpoints and ideas, they may not constrain that funding based on viewpoint or ideology. This principle applies to the scheme of federal tax exemption at issue not only in *Big Mama Rag* but also in a well-known Supreme Court decision, *Bob Jones University v. United States*. And it encompasses the kinds of forums for student organizations on public college and university campuses at issue in the Court's decision in *Christian Legal Society v. Martinez*. Let's call this the "public funding requirement."

CIVIC PRACTICES

Chapters 5–8 canvass the civic practices of confident pluralism that for the most part lie beyond the reach of the law. We can, of course, argue for the importance of constitutional commitments and then ignore the norms underlying those commitments in our own lives. But it is better to reflect our aspirations for the law in the way we live. Embracing confident pluralism in our civic practices can also reinforce our constitutional commitments. This connection between culture and law is one of the key insights of law professor Vincent Blasi's argument that the best way, and perhaps the only way, to strengthen the First Amendment is to ensure that it "evokes genuine sentiments of long-term commitment or aspiration." The civic practices of confident pluralism draw upon similar intuitions.[15]

Chapter 5 introduces three civic aspirations that move us closer toward a world of confident pluralism. *Tolerance* is the recognition that people are for the most part free to pursue their own beliefs and practices, even those beliefs and practices we find morally objectionable. *Humility* takes the further step of recognizing that others will sometimes find our beliefs and practices morally objectionable, and that we can't always "prove" that we are right and they are wrong. *Patience* points toward restraint, persistence, and endurance in our interactions across difference. We can pursue these aspirations without agreeing on the reasons for doing so. If enough of us embrace them, we may be able to sustain confident pluralism even as we disagree about the underlying justifications.

Chapter 6 looks at the implications of confident pluralism for our speech, including our use of name-calling and labeling. The First Amendment's free speech right allows us to say almost anything to almost anyone. But that freedom places a great deal of responsibility on us for what we choose to say. On most of the deeply contested issues at the core of our divisiveness, our efforts toward confident pluralism are especially hindered by two kinds of speech: the hurtful insult and the conversation stopper. Speech that breeds social intolerance by stigmatizing people instead of challenging ideas is at odds with the aspirations of confident pluralism. We can choose to avoid this stigmatizing speech and instead pursue what law professor James Boyd White calls "living speech." Let's call this the "speech imperative."[16]

Chapter 7 considers the role of collective action (including boycotts, strikes, and protests) directed against our fellow citizens. Collective action reveals an inherent and perhaps irresolvable tension for confident pluralism. On the one hand, confident pluralism encourages collective action to resist and challenge forms of majoritarian power. On the other hand, collective action directed at other private citizens and their institutions exerts a kind of power that may be inconsistent with confident pluralism. Chapter 7 explores these tensions by considering a civil rights era boycott in Claiborne County, Mississippi, and the more recent Internet boycott of the Mozilla Corporation over its hiring of Brendan Eich. The aspirations of tolerance, humility, and patience do not point to a bright-line rule for our collective action, but they do offer some guidance. Let's call this the "collective action imperative."

Chapter 8 examines the implications of confident pluralism for our engagement with people who differ from us in important and often insurmountable ways. Those relationships are not always possible—sometimes the best we can do is coexist. But in many cases, we can work together toward common ground in spite of our differences. These common efforts may not actually bridge our ideological differences—we may remain uncompromising or unchanged in our own views. That's not to say that either compromise or change is impossible. But it does suggest that meaningful relationships for the sake of shared interests do not depend on either one. Let's call this the "common ground imperative."

The discussion about civic practices is based as much on experience as it is on expertise. It arises out of some of my own encounters with pluralism and difference—a reminder that none of us speaks from a "neutral" position unencumbered by our backgrounds. Like many people, I would like to think of myself as part of the reasonable middle—patiently (and tolerantly and humbly) waiting for others to move toward my beliefs. But what counts as "the reasonable middle" is usually in the eye of the beholder. Plenty of people on all sides of me will see some of my views as extreme and offensive in one way or another, while others will think that I don't go far enough. And plenty of people will think the same of your views.

Part I

CONSTITUTIONAL COMMITMENTS

CHAPTER 1
OUR MODEST UNITY
RIGHTS, INCLUSION, AND DISSENT

Confident pluralism explores how we might live together in our deep and sometimes painful differences. We should not underestimate the significance of those differences. We lack agreement about the purpose of our country, the nature of the common good, and the meaning of human flourishing. On these questions, Americans are—and perhaps always have been—a deeply divided people.[1]

On the other hand, we do share *some* agreement. For all of our differences, we agree about many of the background practicalities we need to live as a society. Most of us value public roads, national defense, and sewer systems. We agree about many legal functions, like the payment of taxes and the need for courts and prisons. And we also share some constitutional commitments.[2]

We might say that we have a modest unity.

This chapter locates part of our modest unity in a constitutional tradition that gives us a common vocabulary, history, and set of norms. We share a tradition that recognizes the wisdom of limiting state power, of encouraging persuasion over coercion, and of supporting a robust civil society. We share this constitutional heritage, even absent a shared religious or ethnic heritage.

Our modest unity includes two important premises: inclusion and dissent. The inclusion premise is that we are continually reshaping the boundaries of our political community. The dissent premise is that even as we work to extend and renegotiate these boundaries, we recognize the freedom of citizens in the voluntary groups of civil society to differ from established norms. Neither premise is an absolute. Inclusion will stop short of giving toddlers the right to vote or legally insane people the right to bear arms. Dissent will not extend to child molesters or cannibals.

We'll look more carefully at inclusion and dissent at the end of this chapter. But let's turn first to one of the core aspects of our modest unity that emerges from within our constitutional tradition: the individual rights set out in the Bill of Rights.

INDIVIDUAL RIGHTS

When the First Congress debated the wisdom of having a bill of rights, James Madison warned that mere "paper barriers" might fail to secure the liberty of the people against an overreaching majoritarianism. Yet Madison recognized that even paper barriers "have a tendency to impress some degree of respect for them, to establish the public opinion in their favor, and rouse the attention of the whole community." To this end, they "may be one mean to controul the majority from those acts to which they might be otherwise inclined."[3]

Madison's measured optimism has been somewhat vindicated. The individual rights set forth in the Bill of Rights have often guarded our ideas, our groups, and our ways of life from unwarranted state interference. The Second Amendment protects a "right to keep and bear arms." The Fourth, Fifth, and Sixth amendments set important limits on criminal investigations and prosecutions. The Eighth Amendment constrains "cruel and unusual punishments." These protections, to be sure, are uneven, contested, and evolving. But they have amounted to far more than paper barriers.

The check against majoritarian power and the protection from unwarranted state interference are nowhere more evident than in the First Amendment. The First Amendment's expressive and relational protections extend not only to our own interests, but also to ideas and groups that we don't like. We might think of these rights as facilitating a kind of mutual nonaggression pact, placing limits on what the state can do to any of us, for the sake of us all.

These mutually beneficial aspects of the First Amendment anchor some of the Supreme Court's canonical opinions. Consider these memorable words from Justice Louis Brandeis:

> Those who won our independence . . . believed that freedom to think as you will and to speak as you think are means indispensable to the discovery and spread of political truth; that without free speech and assembly discussion would be futile; that with them, discussion affords ordinarily adequate protection against the dissemination of noxious doctrine; that the greatest menace to freedom is an inert people; that public discussion is a political duty; and that this should be a fundamental principle of the American government.[4]

A similar spirit is captured in a well-known passage from Justice Robert Jackson, defending the right of Jehovah's Witnesses to abstain from the pledge of allegiance during the Second World War:

> We apply the limitations of the Constitution with no fear that freedom to be intellectually and spiritually diverse, or even contrary, will disintegrate the social organization. . . . Freedom to differ is not limited to things that do not matter much. That would be a mere shadow of freedom. The test of its substance is the right to differ as to things that touch the heart of the existing order.[5]

The right to differ from orthodoxy transcends any one viewpoint or belief. In the 1940s the Jehovah's Witnesses confronted the orthodoxy of patriotism. In the 1960s civil rights groups stood against the orthodoxy of Jim Crow. In the 1980s gay rights groups challenged the orthodoxy of heterosexuality. Today's orthodoxies have shifted yet again. But we retain the right to differ.

One of the most important protections for this right to differ is today one of the most forgotten: the right of the people "peaceably to assemble." Although the significance of assembly has been lost from public consciousness in recent decades, it remains part of our modest unity even in its current hibernation. For most of our country's history, the right of assembly and the values that animate it have emboldened and protected dissenting and countercultural groups from across the political spectrum. They have created space for the voluntary groups of civil society to challenge prevailing norms and seemingly settled matters of policy.

Let's look more closely at the right of assembly. The First Amendment recognizes "the right of the people peaceably to assemble, and to petition for a redress of grievances." Some scholars have assumed that this wording limits the right of assembly to the purposes of petitioning the government. But a careful examination of text and history confirms that assembly and petition are separate rights. In fact, the broad contours of assembly were present from its constitutional inception. Debates in the House of Representatives during the adoption of the Bill of Rights linked the right of assembly to the arrest and trial of William Penn for an act of religious worship that had nothing to do with petition.[6]

The earliest understandings of assembly also emphasized its importance to protecting unpopular and unorthodox groups. When Thomas Hartley of Pennsylvania proposed limiting the right to groups that assembled for "the general good," Elbridge Gerry of Massachusetts responded that contending for such a right was in fact "contend[ing] for nothing." In other words, the right of assembly could not be limited to "the general good" because it needed to extend to groups that might oppose that conception of the good.[7]

At the end of the eighteenth century, the Democratic-Republican societies emerging out of the increasingly partisan divide between Federalists and Republicans repeatedly insisted on their right to form voluntary groups out of step with prevailing political norms. President George Washington took aim at these societies in his 1794 address to Congress, asserting that "associations of men" and "certain self-created societies" had fostered the Whiskey Rebellion. Historian Irving Brant observes "the damning epithet 'self-created' indorsed the current notion that ordinary people had no right to come together for political purposes."[8]

But "ordinary people" continued to gather in voluntary groups for all kinds of purposes. During the antebellum era, they did so as both free and enslaved blacks. During the Progressive Era, they gathered, marched, and engaged with others for women's rights, civil rights, and labor rights. Law professor Akhil Amar has observed that these kinds of groups brought "a different lived experience" to the words of the First Amendment's assembly clause.[9]

Prominent twentieth-century Americans, including Zechariah Chafee, Louis Brandeis, John Dewey, Orson Welles, and Eleanor Roosevelt all emphasized the significance of the assembly right. During the late 1930s and early 1940s, assembly anchored what were then known as the "Four Freedoms" (which also included speech, press, and religion). At the 1939 World's Fair, journalist Dorothy Thompson delivered a speech on assembly broadcast internationally from Radio City Music Hall. Thompson called assembly "the most essential right of the four." She continued:

> The right to meet together for one purpose or another is actually the guaranty of the three other rights. Because what good is free speech if it is impossible to assemble people to listen to it? How are you going to have discussion at all unless you can hire a hall? How are you going to practice your religion, unless you can meet with a community of people who feel the same way? How can you even get out a newspaper, or any publication, without assembling some people to do it?[10]

The history of assembly suggests that it encompasses more than group expression in momentary gatherings. Assembly extends to the groups that precede expression. This is one of the key insights of assembly that contemporary First Amendment doctrine obscures: in order to protect the expression that emerges from groups and effects political change, we must first protect the background relationships and informal activities that provide the space and structure for that expression to form. As law professor Michael McConnell has asserted:

> Freedom of assembly was understood to protect not only the assembly itself but also the right to organize assemblies through

more or less continual associations and for those associations to select their own members by their own criteria. The Sons of Liberty's public meetings were not purely spontaneous gatherings; they were planned, plotted, and led by men who shared a certain vision and met over a period of time, often secretly, to organize them. In this respect, the freedom of assembly is preparatory to the freedom of speech.[11]

Most assemblies flow out of groups of people who gather to eat, talk, and share ideas long before they make political speeches or enact agendas. Indeed, the vision of assembly encompassing groups that create rather than simply manifest expression facilitates the informal bonds that have strengthened some of our most important social movements. Historians John Hope Franklin and Alfred A. Moss Jr. describe how "moments of informality" spread across clubs, literary parties, and other events created "a cohesive force" among the leaders of the Harlem Renaissance. Early suffragists organized around banner meetings, potato-sack races, baby shows, pageants, and teatimes. Religious movements have relied upon ordinary gatherings like church dinners and small groups. And gay rights groups nurtured relationships and built political strategy through "gay social and activity clubs, retreats, vacations, and professional organizations."[12]

The voluntary groups protected by the right of assembly also foster relationships that enable us to pursue self-realization and self-governance. Law professor Richard Garnett reminds us that these groups provide "alternative sources of meaning and education, and are essential both to genuine pluralism and to freedom of thought and belief." Some bonds, Supreme Court Justice William Brennan has argued, "foster diversity and act as critical buffers between the individual and the power of the State." That solidarity empowers us to challenge, and even to reject, prevailing norms.[13]

The right of assembly reflects goals and purposes different from those underlying the First Amendment's free *speech* right. One of the most important differences is that assembly invokes a relational context: one can speak alone; one cannot assemble alone. A second unique aspect of assembly is that it allows multiple actors to engage not only with an external audience, but also with one another within a group: to foster ideas and identities in the "pre-expressive" moments of group formation. Finally, even as assembly fosters solidarity, it also benefits individuals. Law professor Timothy Zick suggests "the ability to freely assemble or join with others fortifies individuals" and "emboldens them to come forward, and to participate in social and political activities." Thus, Zick notes, "in addition to creating space for group activities and group autonomy, the freedom of assembly facilitates a variety of individual acts of defiance, contention, and expression." These sociological insights are reinforced by examples ranging from coming out experiences to religious rebirths. And the protections for these deeply personal experiences are not intuitively located in the free speech right.[14]

The protections of assembly are part of our mutual nonaggression pact. They extend to groups that we like and groups that we don't like. In the memorable phrase of Supreme Court Justice Hugo Black, "the freedoms of speech, press, petition and assembly guaranteed by the First Amendment must be accorded to the ideas we hate, or sooner or later they will be denied to the ideas we cherish."[15]

RELIGIOUS LIBERTY

Look carefully at Justice Black's quote—something is missing. Black fails to mention the free exercise of religion. The reason for the omission is not clear. It could be that writing in a case about the Communist Party in 1961, Black was focusing on the rights of the First Amendment most relevant to the particular facts. But his omission points to the question of whether religious exercise remains part of our modest unity, and whether it still regarded as beneficial to all.

The suggestion that religious liberty may fall outside of today's modest unity will no doubt unsettle many religious believers. Yet it may be that legal protections for religious free exercise are less salient today than in earlier times. It may be that the free exercise of religion has moved from a right in which all citizens have a stake to a more limited right attractive to only a subset of citizens.

To be sure, the importance of religious freedom as an abstract ideal has not yet lost its cultural and political appeal in the United States. Most Americans value religious liberty in a general sense. And our government continues to advocate for religious freedom around the globe. Consider these words from a 2012 address from then–Secretary of State Hillary Clinton:

> Religious freedom is not just about religion. It's not just about the right of Roman Catholics to organize a mass or Muslims to hold a religious funeral or Baha'is to meet in each other's homes for prayer, or Jews to celebrate high holy days together. As important as those rituals are, religious freedom is also about the right of people to think what they want, say what they think and come together in fellowship without the state looking over their shoulder.[16]

Despite this rhetorical and popular support for religious freedom, fewer people today seem to recognize or care about the immediate need for legal protections rooted in the free exercise of religion. One reason for this change is that many past challenges to religious freedom are no longer active threats. We don't enforce blasphemy laws. We don't compel statements of belief. We don't impose taxes to support the training of ministers. These changes mean that as a practical matter, many Americans no longer depend upon the free exercise right for their religious liberty. They are free to practice their religion without government constraints.[17]

The clearest example—the least threatened religious believer in America today—is the progressively oriented Christian, who at once remains a part of the dominant historical and cultural faith in the United States but whose views are largely aligned with contemporary liberal values. It is hard to think of many aspects of progressive Christian belief and practice that confront government regulation in a way that implicates religious liberty. This is not to say that progressive Christians hold no views antithetical to government interests. For example, many elements of the religious left challenge American policy on war, criminal law, immigration, and the environment. But most of these arguments pose few questions about the boundaries of free exercise—they are religiously informed policy arguments, not religious free exercise arguments.[18]

In addition to progressive religious believers who do not sense an immediate need for legal protections under the free exercise clause, there are also a growing number of Americans who are either actually or functionally *nonreligious*. These nonbelievers are a subset of that opaque and verbally ambiguous category of the "nones"—the survey respondents who signal a lack of any religious affiliation. But unlike merely unaffiliated religious citizens, nonbelievers may have no need for free exercise protections. They are more likely to find affinity with the disestablishment side of the First Amendment's religious liberty protections.[19]

One might think that increased awareness of religious diversity that includes nonbelievers would be reflected in Establishment Clause doctrine. But that has not yet happened. And the Supreme Court's unwillingness to take the interests of nonbelievers more seriously in disestablishment cases further weakens the view that religious liberty benefits all citizens.

One shortcoming of contemporary disestablishment doctrine along these lines is the failure to acknowledge that even "nonsectarian" prayers are incapable of accommodating atheists. In 2014 the Court upheld the constitutionality of prayers offered by private citizens before a local government meeting in the town of Greece, New York. That decision ignores the social realities that now complicate officially sanctioned prayers in ways different from past eras. As Justice Elena Kagan noted in her dissent, these prayers "express beliefs that are fundamental to some, foreign to others—and because that is so they carry the ever-present potential to both exclude and divide."[20]

For all of these reasons, it may be that both nonbelievers and religious progressives will find less significance in the legal protections found under the free exercise clause, particularly when religious liberty claims conflict with other important interests. The possibility of the declining salience of religious liberty is not entirely speculative. During the heated debate surrounding Indiana's religious freedom law in the spring of 2015, some popular commentators began adding scare quotes to the phrase "religious liberty." The debate, which I mentioned in the introduction, focused on business owners who believed their religious commitments precluded them from offering their services for a same-sex wedding. There are good arguments in both directions. It may be that we should follow the lead of Supreme Court Justice William Brennan, who suggested that while commercial businesses are presumptively unprotected by associational freedom, those that can convincingly link their operation to certain causes might receive some level of constitutional protection. On the other hand, we might conclude that religious liberty in commercial settings should be outweighed by other constitutional values like equality. But recognizing competing constitutional values is quite different than questioning the legitimacy of religious liberty itself.[21]

The decline in cultural support for religious liberty illustrated by the Indiana debates is exacerbated by modern legal doctrine around the free exercise clause. The key case is the Supreme Court's 1990 decision, *Employment Division v. Smith*, which held that First Amendment claims rooted in the free exercise of religion receive no special protection against *neutral laws of general applicability*. The problem is that most laws are neutral laws of general applicability. Outside of narrowly drawn exceptions, most laws will withstand challenges grounded in the First Amendment's free exercise right.[22]

One could reasonably view the last twenty-five years of religious liberty law as a patchwork response to *Smith*. The biggest patch, or so it seemed, was the Religious Freedom Restoration Act of 1993 (RFRA), which reinstated a higher level of protection for religious liberty. A subsequent Supreme Court opinion limited the scope of RFRA to action by the federal government. Other state and federal laws followed, but the collective effect of these laws has not undone the damage of *Smith*.[23]

Let me put this a bit more bluntly. Regardless of whether I am right about *cultural* views toward religious liberty, *Smith* has significantly weakened its *legal* dimensions. There are exceptions, including recent decisions favoring religious liberty in *Burwell v.*

Hobby Lobby (limiting mandated employer coverage of contraceptives under the Affordable Care Act) and *Holt v. Hobbs* (invalidating prison regulations prohibiting Muslim inmates from growing short beards). But both of these cases were statutory rather than constitutional decisions. Statutes are limited in jurisdiction—the law in *Hobby Lobby* applies only to the federal government; the law in *Holt* applies only to cases involving prisons and land use. Statutes can also be repealed or amended with greater ease than constitutionally embedded principles.[24]

The decline in cultural and legal support for the free exercise of religion does not mean its functional end, for at least two important reasons. The first is that the Supreme Court continues to recognize some important constitutional protections for religious *groups,* at least insofar as those groups look something like churches or other bodies of worship. The key development in this area of the law is the Court's 2012 decision in *Hosanna-Tabor v. EEOC.* In that case, a unanimous Court recognized a "ministerial exception" to employment discrimination laws. The Court located that exception in the First Amendment's free exercise and establishment clauses.[25]

The justices made clear that the ministerial exception provides an absolute protection for churches to hire and fire ministers. They were less clear about what qualifies as a "church" or who qualifies as a "minister." In addition, the opinion in *Hosanna-Tabor* never really squares the circle with *Smith.* The Court never convincingly explains why *Smith*'s rule about neutral laws of general applicability didn't apply to the neutral law of general applicability at issue in *Hosanna-Tabor.* The protections for religious groups rooted in *Hosanna-Tabor* are thus neither precisely defined nor entirely coherent. But they are real protections, and they mitigate some of the challenges confronting religious free exercise.

The second reason for thinking that continued protections for religion remain part of our modest unity is that religious belief and practice fall squarely within the protections afforded under other First Amendment rights. In fact, religious individuals and groups have long shaped the contours of these other rights. Much of the history of the rights of speech, press, and assembly has been shaped by dissenting religious groups like Quakers, Baptists, Catholics, Mormons, and Jehovah's Witnesses.

Thus, even if the category of religious liberty is losing its cultural and constitutional traction, religious groups and religious expression remain at the core of what we protect through the individual rights guaranteed under the Bill of Rights. They remain an important part of the check against majoritarian power and the ability of individuals to establish meaning apart from government orthodoxy—an important part of our modest unity.[26]

I mentioned at the beginning of this chapter that our modest unity also includes the two premises of inclusion and dissent. Let's look at each of these.

THE INCLUSION PREMISE

The inclusion premise aims for basic membership in the political community to those within our boundaries. The political community at the founding of our country constrained its membership in ways that the current community rightly rejects. The differences between then and now are most readily seen in the ways that today's political community includes blacks and women. There are other changes as well, some of them ongoing. And there may more to come. These are good things. A political community whose membership fails to include the people within its boundaries is not truly pluralistic.

One reason for the inclusion premise is that confident pluralism depends upon both a willingness *and* an ability to partner toward the possibility of mutual coexistence. Too often, the American experiment has denied some people the ability to engage. It was not that long ago that Jim Crow reigned in the South or that wartime hysteria led to mass internment of Japanese Americans.

Consider the story of Lily and Taizo. Educated, middle-class Americans, they in many ways benefited from our modest unity. Taizo graduated from Berkeley in 1929 with a degree in mechanical engineering. He had a good job, and he and Lily started a family in Santa Monica. But in 1942 they lost their property and their freedom when President Roosevelt ordered the internment of Japanese

Americans—three months after he heralded the "immeasurable privileges" of the First Amendment as "the pillars which sustain the temple of liberty under law."[27]

Lily recounts what happened next:

> We started getting letters from the government that told us to get rid of everything we had. We had to go into our savings. We were planning to build a house in Santa Monica, but we had to take out all of our savings. On Tai's birthday, May 17th, we had to go into camp. We were only allowed to take one suitcase apiece, so we couldn't even bring blankets. We boarded a train and headed for Manzanar. When we got there, that was the saddest time. We couldn't even get baby formula. My mother-in-law was in a wheelchair, and we couldn't even push it because the place was so sandy. When we got to our barracks, we were exhausted. I opened the door, and all that was there were a couple of cots and some blankets. I just stood there and cried.

Taizo and Lily spent two years at Manzanar. They were interviewed by the FBI in 1944:

> Tai said that he didn't understand why we were being interned because we had been born in this country, educated in this country, and never even seen Japan. He said that we were citizens and he didn't think we should be interned. The men from Washington told us that everything we had said had to be written down, and because of what Tai had said, we were being sent to Tule Lake. Some of the interviewers couldn't understand why anyone was unhappy here because we were being fed and treated well.

Tule Lake was a higher-security camp—Lily was told it was for "troublemakers." As she noted, "it was more strict and when we got there we behaved well." When Taizo and Lily were finally released at the end of World War II, they left with no possessions, no jobs, and an uncertain future.

I never met my Grandpa Tai. He struggled to make sense of the remnants of his life after the war and died twelve years later at the age of fifty-one. Grandma Lily never remarried. She raised five children in a small home in Palmyra, New Jersey. She died four years ago at the age of ninety-nine. It's fair to say that my grandparents and the 110,000 other Japanese Americans interned alongside them did not enjoy basic membership in the political community. Neither did my father, born at Manzanar in 1943.[28]

It would be foolish to think that simply because we have moved past the injustices of the internment and other egregious civil liberties deprivations that membership in the political community has been secured for everyone. We live in a country with massive disparities in wealth, housing, and access to education, many of them perpetuated along racial lines. We confine hundreds of thousands of immigrants for years in detention centers outside of the public eye. In 2011 alone, the United States held 425,000 immigrants in custody. And we incarcerate a higher proportion of our own citizens than any other country in the world. As commentator Adam Gopnik has observed:

> That city of the confined and the controlled, Lockuptown, is now the second largest in the United States. The accelerating rate of incarceration over the past few decades is just as startling as the number of people jailed: in 1980, there were about two hundred and twenty people incarcerated for every hundred thousand Americans; by 2010, the number had more than tripled, to seven hundred and thirty-one. No other country even approaches that.

Many of the people we send away for years have committed only nonviolent offenses. Many of them—in the federal system, 96 percent of them—go to prison without the benefit of a trial.[29]

These facts suggest serious shortcomings in the realization of the inclusion premise. And that failure doesn't just play out in eye-popping statistics. I teach criminal law at a university seven miles from Ferguson, Missouri, the site of widespread protests in 2014 that drew national attention to problems in the local criminal justice system. Every year I require my students to observe a criminal proceeding in a local courtroom. Every year their stories reflect dismay at the glaring racial disparities and the impersonal wheels of justice. The last courtroom that I visited, just west of Ferguson, was housed in a strip mall. About a hundred defendants—almost all of them without lawyers—sat in rows of metal chairs, waiting for hours to have a brief exchange with a judge who would tell them where they must go next. All of the defendants in that particular courtroom were there on misdemeanor charges for nonviolent crimes. Almost every defendant was black.[30]

While these anecdotes do not by themselves establish that some of my neighbors lack membership in the political community, other investigative work suggests that criminal justice and racial injustice are intrinsically linked in St. Louis and its surrounding municipalities. Those connections point to incredibly complex structural challenges connected to housing, education, and employment. And St. Louis is by no means an isolated example. We could make similar observations of Cleveland, Staten Island, Baltimore, or any one of the hundreds of American cities that confront similar challenges.[31]

Of course, we disagree deeply over the causes of and solutions to these challenges. Many conservatives focus on individual responsibility, while many progressives look to state-centered reforms. Part of our ongoing political debate will be about those causes and those solutions. But in the course of our dialogue, we can at least strive for the common aspiration of extending to others basic membership in the political community.

What might this mean in concrete terms? We could start by prioritizing meaningful access to the basic goods of education, employment, housing, and public accommodations. Consider, for example, the Supreme Court's assertion in *Brown v. Board of Education* that education "is required in the performance of our most basic public responsibilities." Or take the area of employment, where the Court has observed that the purpose of Title VII of the Civil Rights Act of 1964 is "to assure equality of employment opportunities and to eliminate those discriminatory practices and devices which have fostered racially stratified job environments to the disadvantage of minority citizens." Similar rationales justify legally enforced access to housing and public accommodations (although, as I discuss in chapter 3, we lack clarity about the definition of "public accommodation"). These basic requirements are also part of our shared constitutional heritage, another dimension of what should be our modest unity.[32]

THE DISSENT PREMISE

The second premise of our modest unity is that we must be able to reject the norms established by the broader political community within our own lives and voluntary groups. We must be able to dissent. The importance of dissent is well recognized in our constitutional tradition. As Supreme Court Justice William Brennan has argued, "collective effort on behalf of shared goals is especially important in preserving political and cultural diversity and in shielding dissident expression from suppression by the majority." This value of dissent entails risk because it strengthens a genuine pluralism against majoritarian demands for consensus. Today, it resists what political theorist Nancy Rosenblum has called the liberal state's "logic of congruence," which requires "that the internal life and organization of associations mirror liberal democratic principles and practices."[33]

Dissent is not unbounded—every society imposes limits. The philosopher John Stuart Mill's "no harm" principle grossly oversimplifies the calculation of how we draw our lines, but at some point the harms will be so widely acknowledged that individuals and groups perpetuating them will not be tolerated. Almost everyone agrees that we will not allow pedophiles or cannibals or Al Qaeda operatives to live openly in our society. We may make room for some who fantasize about certain actions, but those who actually engage in them are beyond the pale.[34]

Longstanding First Amendment doctrine also allows the state to regulate groups whose practices or advocacy approach the threshold of violence. But the state bears a high burden of drawing the constitutionally appropriate line. The Supreme Court emphasized this burden in a seminal decision almost fifty years ago that established the still-operative limit: "Statutes affecting the right of assembly, like those touching on freedom of speech, must observe the established distinctions between mere advocacy and incitement to imminent lawless action."[35]

Within these limits, the dissent premise will sometimes mean that citizens and the groups that they form will choose to reject the norms of the political community—they may be illiberal or inegalitarian, or they may ignore the civic practices of confident pluralism. A political community that fails to honor the dissent premise is not truly pluralistic—it lacks confidence in itself.

The dissent premise is under pressure from both left and right arguments that attempt to weaken the legitimacy and protections of dissenting groups with ill-defined but rhetorically pleasing concepts like equality, justice, morality, and dignity. The philosopher Alasdair MacIntyre has shown that these concepts abstracted from a particular tradition have no limiting principle—they can be deployed to any political end. And when they are elevated to sacred status in political discourse, they risk upending the dissent premise.[36]

Take the idea of "equality." Equality is a relational concept that can mean nothing on its own. As law professor Steven Smith has noted, its "substantive content must come from other sources." And we can only argue about these other sources when we decide which differences justify different treatment.[37]

To see why this is the case, recall the example of transgender students at Wellesley College that I mentioned in the introduction. The integration of transgender students at a school like Wellesley raises discrete policy questions on topics ranging from bathrooms to sports teams. What is "equal treatment" in these situations, and in which way should accommodations run? Is excluding transgender students from athletic teams unequal treatment of those students, or would their inclusion unequally disadvantage other student-athletes? Would establishing a separate bathroom for transgender students be an adequate accommodation, or would opening all bathrooms to transgender students better reflect equality? Would the latter alternative be "equal treatment" of a conservative Muslim student who chose Wellesley for the security of an all-women's environment? An appeal to an unspecified notion of equality cannot answer these questions.

Shifting the focus to *equality of opportunity* is a step in the right direction, but it will not fully resolve the ambiguity. As political scientist Lawrence Joseph has observed, "just as there is not a single, essential concept of 'equality,' neither is there a single, essential concept of 'equality of opportunity.'" Rather, the meaning of "equality of opportunity" depends on the context in which it is used and "does not, by itself, provide any clear criteria for the distribution of social reward and privileges."[38]

Consider the example of friendships and social networks. Many people would benefit from being invited to the cocktail parties of wealthy and powerful people in Washington, DC, New York, or Los Angeles. We could all make similar claims upon other social networks, from country club memberships to middle school cliques to workplace lunch groups. In each of these cases, some people are given more opportunity than others. In each of these cases, some people lack equality of opportunity. But it would not be possible to determine which social networks were sufficiently open to equality of opportunity, on what basis equality would be measured, or how we would remedy inequalities. That is another reason that civil rights laws have tended to focus on more concrete goals like access to basic goods like education, employment, housing, and public accommodations rather than on unbounded notions of equality.

When we move from specific policy recommendations to free-floating appeals to equality (or justice, morality, or dignity), we undermine the dissent premise. Almost seventy years ago, the English novelist George Orwell flagged this worry, noting that words like "equality" have "several different meanings which cannot be reconciled with one another." In a 1946 essay titled "Politics and the English Language," Orwell wrote that when it comes to certain political topics, "the concrete melts into the abstract and no one seems able to think of turns of speech that are not hackneyed: prose consists less and less of words chosen for the sake of their meaning, and more and more of phrases tacked together like the sections of a prefabricated henhouse." Words without content will find their meaning in majoritarian ideas.[39]

KEEPING FAITH

The precise contours of inclusion and dissent are contested, and they will remain so. Negotiating and renegotiating these premises strains our modest unity. Moreover, the fact that we must recognize inevitable limits on both inclusion and dissent reminds us that political solutions always require tradeoffs and compromises. It will not be possible to fully realize these premises, which is also to say that it will not be possible to fully realize confident pluralism. That reality introduces a note of inevitable tragedy to our attempts to live with one another.[40]

Recognizing a tragic dimension to our efforts at peaceful coexistence does not mean that we are chasing windmills. The theologian Reinhold Niebuhr once observed that "democracy is a method of finding proximate solutions to insoluble problems." The same could be said of the constitutional commitments and civic practices of confident pluralism. Let's turn first to the constitutional commitments.[41]

CHAPTER 2

THE VOLUNTARY GROUPS REQUIREMENT
REHABILITATING THE RIGHT OF ASSOCIATION

The First Amendment provides that "Congress shall make no law respecting an establishment of religion, or prohibiting the free exercise thereof; or abridging the freedom of speech, or of the press; or the right of the people peaceably to assemble, and to petition the government for a redress of grievances." Look carefully at the text. It contains five individual rights: speech, press, assembly, petition, and the free exercise of religion. As one Supreme Court opinion observed, these rights are "interwoven" with one another. They have distinct but mutually reinforcing purposes.[1]

Recent constitutional decisions have obscured these connections. They have collapsed the right *to form groups* under the assembly clause down to the right *to speak* under the free speech clause. One misstep contributing to this collapse is the judicially recognized right of association. Look again at the text of the First Amendment—you will not find a right of association there, and you will not find it anywhere else in the text of the Constitution. Another misstep came with the Court's conclusion that sometimes the right of association simply "merges" with the free speech right, rendering the former constitutionally redundant.[2]

Shifting the constitutional focus exclusively to speech neglects the protections for group formation and activity, and the history behind those protections. There is a reason that our modest unity includes a healthy dose of skepticism about the ability of government to respect the boundaries of nonconforming groups. A focus on free speech that neglects this wisdom falls short of our constitutional commitments. Confident pluralism cannot happen without meaningful protections for voluntary groups.

The law surrounding the right of association is plagued with problems of its own. Twenty-six years after first recognizing this right, the Court split it into two flavors: *intimate association* and *expressive association*. According to the Court, intimate association is an "intrinsic" feature of the right of association that focuses on "highly personal relationships" and "deep attachments and commitments." This sounds promising, but courts have drawn its limits quite narrowly. In practical terms, intimate association extends only to close family relationships—courts have refused to extend its protections even to small social groups or tightly knit religious groups. And the close family relationships that qualify as intimate associations are already well protected under separate constitutional protections—the Supreme Court has long recognized special protections for spousal and parent-child relationships. For this reason, the right of intimate association turns out to be almost meaningless. It fails to offer any real protections to any real groups that are not already constitutionally protected by other means. In other words, the right of intimate association adds almost nothing to the balance of our civil liberties.[3]

The right of expressive association also comes up short. The basic idea of expressive association is that a group is eligible for constitutional protection only to the extent that its purposes and activities further some other First Amendment interest, such as speech, press, or religion. The Supreme Court has put it this way: "implicit in the right to engage in activities protected by the First Amendment" is "a corresponding right to associate with others in pursuit of a wide variety of political, social, economic, educational, religious, and cultural ends."[4]

In other words, the legal doctrine of expressive association *instrumentalizes* the associational right—it must be enlisted toward some purportedly more significant end. But as political theorist George Kateb has observed, in the real world "people find in association a value in itself." When people associate, they "discover numerous sorts of pleasure apart from the pleasure of success in their specific pursuits." Kateb focuses not on intimacy, but rather on "relationships less intense, more limited, sometimes more casual or episodic or artificial." He properly emphasizes that "these relationships have their own worth." Instrumentalizing association toward outwardly expressive ends neglects these other goods.[5]

Expressive association also comes with a troubling corollary: some associations are considered to be "nonexpressive." This category of nonexpressive association obscures the fact that all associative acts have expressive potential: joining, gathering, speaking, and not speaking can all be expressive. It becomes very difficult, if not impossible, to police this line apart from the expressive intent of the members of the group. And many groups that might at first blush seem to be nonexpressive could in fact articulate an expressive intent.

The legal consequences of the distinction between expressive and nonexpressive are striking. A law restricting a nonexpressive association faces almost no constitutional obstacles—it need only pass "rational basis" scrutiny, and almost any law will meet this threshold. That means that a voluntary group deemed nonexpressive could be regulated if a state or local government concludes that the group's membership requirements are out of step with majoritarian norms, if elected officials want to promote public order or discretionary zoning preferences, or if law enforcement officials want to limit the size or composition of the group for purposes of crowd control. Let's look at an example.

THE TOP HATTERS

The Top Hatters Motorcycle Club is a California biker group founded by brothers Jess and Joe Bravo in 1947. Members focus most of their time on "club functions that benefit our community." Their "number one priority" is "riding and strengthening our brotherhood in the biker community." The club also "maintains a strong regard for family, brotherhood and motorcycling."[6]

The original Top Hatters chapter is located in Hollister, fifteen

miles south of Gilroy. Most people haven't heard of Gilroy, but at
different times in its history the town has been known as the Hay
and Grain Capital of California, the Dairy and Cheese Capital of
California, and the Tobacco Capital of the United States. Today it is
known as the Garlic Capital of the World. True to its modern heritage, the town has hosted the annual Gilroy Garlic Festival since
1979, which draws tens of thousands of participants.[7]

On July 30, 2000, four Top Hatters from the Hollister chapter
rode north to the garlic festival to celebrate member Bob Poekler's
birthday. Bob and his Top Hatter brothers arrived wearing leather
and denim vests bearing the club's insignia: a skull with wings
wearing a top hat. Gilroy Police Sergeant Don Kludt approached
the four men and told them that their "gang colors" violated the
festival's (unwritten) dress code. When the Top Hatters protested,
Sergeant Kludt called for backup and escorted the four bikers out
of the Gilroy Garlic Festival.[8]

The Top Hatters sued the town of Gilroy and the festival organizers, alleging violations of their First Amendment rights of speech
and expressive association. A federal judge rejected their claims,
concluding that the Top Hatters' vests expressed no message and
that a motorcycle club did not qualify as an expressive association.
On appeal, the Top Hatters noted with some irony that the trial
judge had found their vests lacked a message, even though the festival organizers had ejected them precisely because of the message
of their vests. The group also argued that they qualified as an expressive association. A federal appeals court rejected both claims.[9]

Let's focus on the legal conclusion that the Top Hatters is "nonexpressive." Does it pass the test of common sense? The Top Hatters make no secret that they are "not for everyone." They limit their
group to "exclusively Harley Davidson motorcycles," and insist
that they "will stay that way until the end of time." They bill themselves as "a strong brotherhood of only serious motorcycle riders,"
and caution: "We are not a social, weekender riding club, we are
a brotherhood of bikers that take riding and flying our colors very
serious."[10]

The Top Hatters express all kinds of things in their membership boundaries. They *embrace* their members, and they *exclude* everyone else, even those who might really want to join their group and who are hurt by their exclusion. The Top Hatters maintain their boundaries over time according to their own standards. If a member drifts from the group's values, beliefs, or norms—say, takes a sudden liking to Yamahas—the club's other members might debate whether he is still a "real Top Hatter." If they conclude that Yamahas don't cut it for Top Hatters, they might *expel* the wayward member. Those who remain in the group would *establish* the Top Hatters through their riding, but also through their relationships with one another. Each of these actions of embrace, exclusion, expulsion, and establishment shapes the contours of the Top Hatters. These actions are also expressive—they create social meaning for the members of the Top Hatters, and also for those left out.

Along the way, the Top Hatters' purposes might grow beyond what they ever imagined. For example, they might discover not only a shared love of the Harley Davidson Night Train, but also a common passion for the public schools in Hollister. Some of the group's members might form deep friendships that lead to business ventures or social activism. Of course, the Top Hatters might do nothing more than ride motorcycles together. We do not know what will develop out of their group and the relationships that form within it. But if we wait until the group satisfies some vague judicial standard of "expressiveness," we may never know.

The Top Hatters also have a website: www.tophatters-mc.com. The website certainly looks like it is expressing all kinds of things. Its home page provided most of the quotes in the first paragraph of this section. The "Photos" section displays pictures from past rides, parties, and picnics. Click on the "Jukebox" page and you will hear the group's favorite songs, including the Rolling Stones' "Paint it Black" and the Doors' "Break On Through." The "Memorial" page is a photo tribute to a deceased member, William H. Alnas, with the caption: "RIDE FOREVER FREE WILLIE! YOU WILL BE IN EVERYBODY'S HEART! TOP HATTERS BROTHER FOREVER!" If we were to try to evaluate whether the Top Hatters was sufficiently "expressive" in light of its website, how would we know and whom would we ask? On what basis would we conclude that the Top Hatters memorial page, pictures, and home page are not expressive?[11]

You might celebrate the Top Hatters, or you might bristle at them. The important point is that they have almost no constitutional protection under current doctrine. They lost a federal case because they were deemed "nonexpressive." It's not that the court decided that the government's interest in ensuring a certain decorum at the garlic festival outweighed the Top Hatters' constitutional right of expressive association. Instead, the court sidestepped that balancing analysis altogether by refusing to recognize the group as expressive. Courts have done the same to a number of other groups, including fraternities, social clubs, skating rinks—even a nudist colony.[12]

Here is another example of how the right of expressive association falls short.

THE MUSLIM STUDENTS ASSOCIATION

Jawad Rasul's April 2008 weekend excursion was not unlike that of many college students. A twenty-year-old sophomore at the City College of New York, Jawad and seventeen friends embarked on a whitewater rafting adventure in upstate New York. Part of the Muslim Students Association (MSA) at City College, Jawad had immigrated to the United States after being born in Pakistan. When he first applied for naturalization, his application went nowhere for four years. Then a friend suggested that he write his congressman, and a month later he received an interview and became a citizen. Jawad recounts that the experience made him a "believer" in the democratic process.[13]

As with many student groups, MSA members came and went, and not everyone on the rafting trip knew each other. As it turned out, one of the participants was an undercover informant for the New York Police Department. On April 21, 2008, the informant filed his report on the weekend excursion: "In addition to the regularly scheduled events (rafting), the group prayed at least four times a day, and much of the conversation was spent discussing Islam and was religious in nature."[14]

Jawad first learned the truth when an Associated Press reporter called to break the news. The AP's investigative reporting discovered that the NYPD had placed informants or undercover officers in the MSAs at eight colleges and universities in New York City. In addition, the Department's Cyber Intelligence Unit had regularly monitored the websites, blogs, and forums of MSAs on fifteen other campuses, many of them outside the city's jurisdiction. The unit filed weekly reports that included the names of Muslim students who invited speakers to campus or organized events.[15]

The NYPD's monitoring and surveillance devastated the students in the MSAs. Days after the AP report, nineteen-year-old Micha Balon saw a sign posted at her regular meeting place at Hunter College: "Please refrain from having political conversations in MSA." A leader for one of the MSAs noted that following the news of the AP investigation, "the students wouldn't come to the prayer room. They felt they couldn't meet in their own space." A report coauthored by the Muslim American Civil Liberties Coalition noted bleakly: "American Muslim interviewees stress that the ever-present surveillance chills—or completely silences—their speech whether they are engaging in political debate, commenting on current events, encouraging community mobilization or joking around with friends." The report concluded that "the NYPD's surveillance of students chilled First Amendment activity in what is perhaps the single most important formative and expressive space for any American youth: the college campus."[16]

The NYPD discontinued one of its investigative units in 2014, but several others remain operational. It is possible that a legal challenge could find the NYPD's monitoring a constitutional violation of the Fourth Amendment's constraints on criminal investigations. But it is unlikely that the *First* Amendment would have protected Jawad and the MSA.[17]

This lack of protection comes at a cost. One of those costs is neglecting the longstanding doctrine that aims to provide breathing room for open discussion and uninhibited debate without being "chilled" by the threat of government monitoring. As my colleague Neil Richards has argued, courts should not "cast surveillance as solely a Fourth Amendment issue of crime prevention, rather than as one that also threatens intellectual freedom and First Amendment values of the highest order." Professor Richards writes in the context of electronic surveillance like that undertaken by the NYPD's cyber-surveillance unit. The physical infiltration of a group by an imposter masquerading as an insider adds another First Amendment cost: it betrays trust among members and threatens the internal cohesion of the group. And the right of expressive association arguably fails to protect the MSAs from any of these harms.[18]

THE STRANGE HISTORY OF THE RIGHT OF ASSOCIATION

How can it be that the MSAs might lack any protections against surveillance and infiltration under the right of expressive association? The answer lies partly in the genesis of that right. The Supreme Court first recognized a right of association in 1958, initially linking it to both the rights of speech and assembly. But the Court's earliest efforts to define the contours of the associational right were marred with imprecision and ambiguity. Many of the doctrinal problems emerged because the Court was wrestling with extending associational protections to the National Association for the Advancement of Colored People while at the same time denying those protections to the Communist Party of the United States of America. As legal scholar Harry Kalven quipped at the time, "The Communists cannot win, the NAACP cannot lose." Plagued by the resulting doctrinal tensions, the Court's early association cases began to focus more on *speech* than on the *groups* that enabled expression.[19]

Subsequent courts and scholars doubled down on this mistake. One important example, which I mentioned earlier in this chapter, is the Supreme Court's focus on intimate and expressive association. Those distinctions originated in a 1984 decision involving a charitable organization called the United States Jaycees. The Jaycees sought to provide young men with an "opportunity for personal development and achievement and an avenue for intelligent participation by young men in the affairs of their community, state and nation, and to develop true friendship and understanding among young men of all nations." Like many voluntary groups, the

Jaycees engaged in a diverse array of social, charitable, and political activities. They held parties, led a fundraising drive to combat multiple sclerosis, hosted a women's professional golf tournament, debated issues of public policy, and communicated with local, state, and national officials.[20]

By the mid-1970s, the Jaycees had begun admitting women as "associate" members but restricted them from having full membership rights. The local chapters in Minneapolis and St. Paul started admitting women as regular members, in violation of the national organization's bylaws. After the national organization threatened to revoke their charters, the two Minnesota chapters filed discrimination charges with the Minnesota Department of Human Rights. They based the charges on Minnesota's Human Rights Act, which declared that it was an unfair discriminatory practice "to deny any person the full and equal enjoyment of the goods, services, facilities, privileges, advantages, and accommodations of a place of public accommodation because of race, color, creed, religion, disability, national origin or sex."[21]

In response, members of the national organization filed suit alleging that the Minnesota law violated their rights of speech and association. They argued that Minnesota's actions "would effectively destroy the Jaycees' ability to achieve its core purpose, namely, furthering the interest of young men." The Jaycees asserted that they "would no longer be able to confine the central reason for its existence to the advancement of the interest of young men." They also noted "the power to change the membership of a bona fide private association is unavoidably the power to change its purpose, its programs, its ideology, and its collective voice."[22]

The Supreme Court determined that the Jaycees was an expressive association. But in light of "Minnesota's compelling interest in eradicating discrimination against its female citizens," the Court decided that the expressive association claim failed. Curiously, the Court made no effort to explain how the state's interest in *eradicating* discrimination outweighed the group's associational interests. It is possible that the government interest should have prevailed—if, for example, the Jaycees' level of associate membership significantly inhibited women's access to employment opportunities. But the Court's lack of analysis leaves us without an answer to that question. And the consequence of the Court's decision should not be stated euphemistically: it meant that the all-male Jaycees could no longer exist.[23]

One of the most peculiar aspects of the *Jaycees* opinion is its failure to acknowledge the tension between the right of association and the government's interest in "eradicating" discrimination. As the Court noted elsewhere in its opinion:

> There can be no clearer example of an intrusion into the internal structure or affairs of an association than a regulation that forces the group to accept members it does not desire. Such a regulation may impair the ability of the original members to express only those views that brought them together. Freedom of association therefore plainly presupposes a freedom not to associate.[24]

At least part of the right of association entails discrimination—a meaningful right of association will permit voluntary groups to exclude. The Jaycees discriminated against women. Wellesley College discriminates against men and low-performing high school students. The Mormon Tabernacle Choir discriminates against non-Mormons and bad singers.

Sometimes discrimination is a good thing. Elite universities would not be able to function if they had to accept anyone who wanted to attend. Professional choirs need to limit their vocalists to people who can carry a tune. And within the voluntary groups of civil society, we tolerate even some forms of discrimination that would elsewhere be impermissible. We would be rightly outraged if the federal government discriminated on the basis of gender or religion. But we allow Wellesley College to exclude men, and we allow the Mormon Tabernacle Choir to exclude non-Mormons.

Not all discrimination is legally permissible. But the right of association is an important check against government attempts to impose its own norms. It is essential that courts undertake the analysis and weighing of values that the right of association requires.

The government's interest in eradicating discrimination is not always a sufficient justification to overcome the right of expressive association. In 2000 the Boy Scouts raised an expressive association claim to challenge New Jersey's efforts to force them to retain a gay scoutmaster. In a 5-4 decision, the Supreme Court concluded that the Scouts' expressive association claim prevailed. In this case, the Boy Scouts' right of expressive association permitted them to exclude a gay scoutmaster.[25]

The *Boy Scouts* decision is viewed by some scholars as a strong endorsement of the right of expressive association. Indeed, Chief Justice William Rehnquist's opinion for the five-justice majority deferred to the Scouts' interpretation of their expressive message and forcefully asserted: "It is not the role of the courts to reject a group's expressed values because they disagree with those values or find them internally inconsistent." But the case is not as significant as some commentators suggest.[26]

One weakness of the *Boy Scouts* decision is that it is difficult to reconcile with the *Jaycees* decision, unless the Court simply viewed gender discrimination in 1984 as more important than sexual orientation discrimination in 2000. As Justice John Paul Stevens noted in dissent, the *Jaycees* decision had "squarely held that a State's antidiscrimination law does not violate a group's right to associate simply because the law conflicts with that group's exclusionary membership policy." A number of prominent legal scholars have embraced Stevens's critique. Law professors Andrew Koppelman and Tobias Barrington Wolff have even written a book subtitled "How the Case of *Boy Scouts of America v. James Dale* Warped the Law of Free Association."[27]

We might also wonder if the Court would reach the same conclusion about the Scouts today, when views about sexual orientation discrimination are in a much different place than they were fifteen years ago. Indeed, some people would argue that these changing views are precisely the reason that the *Boy Scouts* decision should come out differently today. But confident pluralism usually cuts in the opposite direction: it protects dissenting viewpoints and the groups that advocate them from forced compliance with majoritarian norms.

It should come as no surprise that constitutional protections for voluntary groups might benefit those groups with less mainstream views. A generation ago, when views on sexual orientation were quite different, gay rights groups found sanctuary in similar protections. In 1974 a federal appellate court rightly sided with a gay student group against the University of New Hampshire's efforts to shut it down. In fact, "in an earlier era, public universities frequently attempted to bar gay rights groups from recognized student organization status on account of their supposed encouragement of what was then illegal behavior. The courts made short shrift of those policies." Law professor Dale Carpenter has similarly observed that "the rise of gay equality and public visibility coincided—not coincidentally, however—with the rise of vigorous protection for First Amendment freedom, especially the freedom of association."[28]

This associational freedom included the freedom not to associate. As Professor Carpenter notes, gay organizations "historically discriminated in membership based on sexual orientation" and "relied on exclusively gay environments in which to feel safe, to build relationships, and to develop political strategy." In fact, "even groups that are not exclusively gay would resist having heterosexuals in leadership positions." Carpenter argues that any exclusionary membership policy "is expressive in just this way." Today's expressive association doctrine has forgotten these perspectives.[29]

RELIGIOUS ASSOCIATIONS

How do religious groups fare under the right of expressive association? You might think that religious groups qualify as expressive because they meet the *Jaycees* requirement that members "associate for the purpose of engaging in those activities protected by the First Amendment—speech, assembly, petition for the redress of grievances, *and the exercise of religion.*" The wrinkle in this analysis is the *Smith* rule that I mentioned in the previous chapter: First

Amendment claims rooted in the free exercise of religion receive no special protection against *neutral laws of general applicability.* Outside of narrowly drawn exceptions, most laws will withstand challenges grounded in the First Amendment's free exercise right. And it seems unlikely that a constitutional framework unwilling to protect a group's religious exercise would nevertheless be willing to protect the group's ability to associate for the purpose of that religious exercise.[30]

Another problem with the current doctrine of expressive association is illustrated in *Christian Legal Society v. Martinez,* the decision upholding the "all-comers" policy at a public law school that I mentioned in the introduction. After the law school refused to recognize a Christian student group that required its members and leaders to adhere to certain belief and conduct requirements, the group argued that its exclusion from the forum of student organizations was constitutionally impermissible. It raised separate claims based on the rights of free speech and expressive association. But the Supreme Court concluded that the two claims "merged." It contended that "expressive association in this case is the functional equivalent of speech itself," which set up the idea that the right of association raised no important values left unaddressed by the free speech right. The clear implication was that association added *nothing* to speech. If that is correct, then a claim that fails on speech grounds will inevitably lose on expressive association grounds. In other words, under the logic of the *Christian Legal Society* decision, whether a group even qualifies as an expressive association is in some cases irrelevant.[31]

Some parts of the law push in a different direction. As I mentioned in the last chapter, the strongest constitutional protections for religious groups arise out of the ministerial exception recognized in *Hosanna-Tabor.* The right of a religious group to select its leaders and members on religious grounds is also reinforced by federal statutes and other Supreme Court decisions. Those protections embrace the view that at least some religious groups can make membership and leadership decisions on the basis of religious belief. They suggest, for example, that a Catholic charity could refuse to hire a Muslim social worker or that a Jewish student group could deny membership to a Methodist.[32]

But the *Christian Legal Society* decision cuts the other way. It endorses the idea that the government can require private groups—including religious ones—to accept "all comers" as a condition of eligibility for access to generally available public benefits. Two recent federal appellate opinions echo this reasoning. In one case, the court concluded that a high school Bible club's requirement that its members "possess a true desire to . . . grow in a relationship with Jesus Christ" violated a school district's nondiscrimination policies because the club's requirement "inherently excludes non-Christians." Four years later, the same court relied on the *Christian Legal Society* case to suggest that a public university might deny official recognition to Christian student groups that limit "their members and officers [to those who] profess a specific religious belief, namely, Christianity."[33]

The Supreme Court may one day try to reconcile *Christian Legal Society* with *Hosanna-Tabor* by drawing distinctions between churches and religious student groups, or between ministers and nonministers. But these distinctions will not hold indefinitely—the Court's two approaches to the constitutional boundaries of religious groups appear to be on a collision course. Consider, for example, a Baptist campus ministry run out of a Baptist church at a public university that adopts an all-comers policy. Suppose this particular Baptist church believes that every member is a minister of the gospel, and while anyone is welcome to attend the group's events, only those who adhere to the church's creeds and ministerial requirements can join the group. How does that case come out under *Hosanna-Tabor*? How does it come out under *Christian Legal Society*? It is not clear that both lines of analysis can hold.[34]

THE VOLUNTARY GROUPS REQUIREMENT

Our voluntary groups are the cornerstone of confident pluralism. The speech and discourse through which we engage with one another depends upon the groups in which we forge ideas, relationships, and affections. And the doctrinal framework that ensures these protections is buckling. In particular, the current right of expressive association fails to offer even minimal protections for "nonexpressive" voluntary groups, and it falls short of providing meaningful protections for many of the groups that do manage to reach its expressive threshold.

The distinction between expressive and nonexpressive is not in the Constitution. Neither, for that matter, is the right of association. I have argued in an earlier book that the right of assembly better anchors the constitutional framework for understanding the boundaries of voluntary groups. But whether through assembly or some reimagined form of association, we need our courts to recognize something like the voluntary groups requirement:

> Government officials should not interfere with the membership, leadership, or internal practices of a voluntary group absent a clearly articulated and precisely defined compelling interest.

The government's interest should be tied to specific harms or credible threats rather than to vague invocations of broadly stated government interests. This kind of specificity does not mean an absolute shield for voluntary groups. For example, when those groups engage in violent activity (like the shootout between rival motorcycle gangs that left nine dead in Waco, Texas, in the spring of 2015), they are appropriately investigated and prosecuted by law enforcement. Similarly, if law enforcement has credible information that a voluntary group is planning criminal activity, it should be able to use appropriate means of monitoring and surveillance. But the specificity of the government interest is important—it should not be abstracted to unchecked levels like those found in the NYPD's surveillance and monitoring of MSAs. Nor should the process of evaluating the government's interest be completely sidestepped with a threshold determination that a group is "nonexpressive," as courts did with the Top Hatters.[35]

The current doctrinal framework needs to change. But merely protecting these groups—merely walling off private spaces from government interference—is not enough. Confident pluralism also invites us to engage with one another across our differences, and in the public square. And it asks that government protect the forums that make that engagement possible. That argument is the subject of the next chapter. It begins with one of my favorite television shows.

CHAPTER 3

THe PUBLIC FORUM RequIRemenT
PUBLIC SPACES, PRIVATE FORUMS, AND
PARKS & RECREATION

The storyline of the hit sitcom *Parks & Recreation* revolves around Leslie Knope and her colleagues in a small government office in the fictional town of Pawnee, Indiana. With the brilliant acting of Amy Poehler and her costars, the show has reached a wide audience over the past few years. *Parks & Recreation* illustrates a number of commonplace government practices, but for our purposes the most important is the public forum. Every few episodes, Leslie and her colleagues host a gathering for Pawnee citizens to discuss and debate some issue of comic insignificance. Like many of the vignettes in *Parks & Recreation*, the show's portrayal of the public forum reflects an actual government practice, in this case one that is grounded in a constitutional doctrine.

THE PUBLIC FORUM DOCTRINE

The public forum doctrine ensures that the government provides spaces where viewpoints can become voices. Public forums can be actual places, like town halls, but they can also be nonphysical or virtual spaces. Public colleges and universities create public forums when they allow students to form their own organizations; local governments often create public forums when they solicit comments on a website.[1]

Sometimes the government opens its property for certain defined expressive purposes. These are called *limited public forums*. They can be limited to a particular class of people (like students on public university campuses) or to a particular topic (like a public hearing on a proposed policy). Limited public forums facilitate confident pluralism by inviting different perspectives on contested issues or goals.[2]

Other public forums are more open: they are places for citizens to raise, develop, and discuss any issue of their choosing. These are called *traditional public forums*. They include streets, parks, and sidewalks. The participants in those forums sometimes speak to government officials. But more often, they speak to other citizens, to the broader public, or even to themselves. These spaces are important to the living out of confident pluralism—as religion scholar Diana Eck has suggested, "pluralism requires the cultivation of public space where we all encounter one another."[3]

One of the reasons that we can laugh at the public forums in *Parks & Recreation* is that most of them focus on issues irrelevant to almost all of us: establishing the state's smallest park, honoring a dead miniature horse named "Little Sebastian," or installing a new bike rack in Pawnee. Occasionally the issues cut a little closer to home, like a proposed ban on oversized sugary soft drinks from Pawnee's local candy manufacturer, Sweetums.

Whether the topic is plausible or absurd, almost every public forum in *Parks & Recreation* devolves into a fracas that displays the inefficiencies and inconveniences that often plague government-sponsored discussions. As Leslie's libertarian boss, Ron Swanson, comments during one of the forums: "This forum, like all public forums, is a waste of time."[4]

Ron has a point. Many public forums *are* a waste of time. Some are even worse—they facilitate harm. For example, most people who have attended a public college or university have witnessed the bizarre and hurtful antics of "street preachers," who hurl insults at passersby in their efforts to expound repentance and salvation. Their platform—including the harm that comes from it—is made possible by the public forum. Public forums introduce costs ranging from serious inefficiencies to serious harms. But they are also vital to a pluralistic society.

Consider a traditional public forum like a city park, with its fields, benches, sidewalks, and playgrounds. The city government owns and manages the land and the physical structures built upon it. But within this space, anyone can say almost anything. Skaters, vagabonds, hipsters, Klansmen, lesbians, Christians, and cowboys— the city park accommodates them all. The city park thus symbolizes a core feature of a democracy: the freedom of all citizens to express their views in public spaces free from the constraints of government-imposed orthodoxy. It reflects what the Supreme Court has repeatedly called our "profound national commitment to the principle that debate on public issues should be uninhibited, robust, and wide-open."[5]

The *ideal* of the public forum represents one of the most important aspects of a healthy democracy. It signifies a willingness to tolerate dissent, discomfort, and even instability. These intuitive connections are not lost on the writers of *Parks & Recreation*. When a delegation from a Venezuelan parks and recreation department visits Pawnee, their leader, Raul, expresses dismay upon observing a public forum: "This is outrageous. Where are the armed men who come in to take the protesters away? Where are they? This kind of behavior is never tolerated in Boraqua. You shout like that, they put you in jail. Right away. No trial, no nothing. Journalists, we have a special jail for journalists."[6]

Sadly, we are not as far from Raul's vision as we might like to believe. Take the events in Ferguson, Missouri. In the fall of 2014 protesters took to the streets in Ferguson following the shooting death of a black teenager, Michael Brown, by a white police officer. The ensuing protests spanned several months. They were complex and varied. Some of them involved violence and callous disregard for law enforcement. But the *initial* protests were largely peaceful, and local law enforcement responded to them with an overwhelming show of force that looked more like a combat operation than crowd control. Police dressed in camouflage fatigues aimed assault rifles on protesters from atop armored personnel carriers. They invented arbitrary rules to keep protesters from assembling. They fired tear gas without sufficient warning. Some officers shouted insults and threats at protesters. And when national and international journalists showed up to cover the protests, police tear-gassed an *Al Jazeera America* news crew and arrested a *Washington Post* reporter.[7]

The police action against protesters and journalists in Ferguson is only one example of the ongoing violations of the public forum in this country. Under current law, political protesters assembling in public forums are often relegated to physically distant and ironically named "free speech zones." Labor picketers confront oppressive restrictions against their practices in public areas. Anti-abortion protesters are banned from public sidewalks.[8]

These violations of the public forum call to mind the words of Dr. Martin Luther King Jr., spoken from the height of the civil rights era:

> If I lived in China or even Russia, or any totalitarian country, maybe I could understand some of these illegal injunctions. Maybe I could understand the denial of certain basic First Amendment privileges, because they hadn't committed themselves to that over there. But somewhere I read of the freedom of assembly. Somewhere I read of the freedom of speech. Somewhere I read of the freedom of press. Somewhere I read that the greatness of America is the right to protest for right.

The public forum in practice is quite unrecognizable from its ideal, and that departure should give us great pause.[9]

DOCTRINAL PROBLEMS

It may seem odd that we see so many constraints on expression in traditional public forums in light of today's generally permissive First Amendment landscape. In recent years, the Supreme Court has upheld the First Amendment rights of video gamers, liars, and people with weird animal fetishes. But in most cases involving the public forum—cases where speech and assembly might actually matter to public discourse and social change—courts have been far less protective of civil liberties.[10]

Part of the reason for this more tepid judicial treatment of the public forum is a formalistic doctrinal analysis that has emerged over the past half-century. Courts allow governmental actors to impose *time, place, and manner* restrictions in public forums. These restrictions must be "reasonable" and "neutral," and they must "leave open ample alternative channels for communication of the information."[11]

The reasonableness requirement is an inherently squishy standard that can almost always be met. The neutrality requirement means that restrictions on a public forum must avoid singling out a particular topic or viewpoint. For example, they cannot limit only political speech or only religious speech (content-based restrictions). And they cannot limit only political speech expressing Republican values or only religious speech expressing Jewish beliefs (viewpoint-based restrictions). It turns out to be pretty easy for government officials to satisfy the neutrality requirement.[12]

The requirement of "ample alternative channels" introduces another highly subjective standard. Lower courts have found that an alternative is not sufficiently ample "if the speaker is not permitted to reach the intended audience" or if the distance between speaker and audience is so great that only those "with the sharpest eyesight and most acute hearing have any chance of getting the message." But the ampleness standard is otherwise underspecified. At least one federal appellate court has concluded that an alternative venue need not be within "sight and sound" of the intended audience.[13]

The Supreme Court's only recent consideration of the ampleness standard came in its deeply divided opinion in *Hill v. Colorado*, which upheld a public forum restriction that had been challenged by anti-abortion protesters. The majority opinion concluded that the restriction left open "ample alternative channels for communication" and did "not entirely foreclose any means of communication." Justice Anthony Kennedy warned in dissent that "our foundational First Amendment cases are based on the recognition that citizens, subject to rare exceptions, must be able to discuss issues, great or small, through the means of expression they deem best suited to their purpose." Kennedy insisted "it is for the speaker, not the government, to choose the best means of expressing a message." That sentiment echoes Justice William Brennan's assertion in an earlier case: "The government, even with the purest of motives, may not substitute its judgment as to how best to speak for that of speakers and listeners; free and robust debate cannot thrive if directed by the government." The underspecified ampleness standard can substantially hinder these goals.[14]

As long as the requirements of reasonableness, neutrality, and ample alternative channels are met, officials can limit the duration and time of day when public forums can be used, the location of an expressive event, and the way in which ideas are conveyed. In principle, these restrictions make sense. In practice, they have been used to control and mute expression and voice.

Consider, for example, how restrictions on *time* can sever the link between message and moment. Closing a public forum for periods of time that encompassed symbolic days of the year like September 11, August 6 (the day the United States detonated an atomic bomb on the city of Hiroshima), or June 28 (the anniversary of the Stonewall Riots) could stifle political dissent. Time restrictions that closed the public sidewalks outside of prisons on days of executions, outside of legislative buildings on days of votes, or outside of courthouses on days that decisions are announced, would raise similar concerns. Yet all of these restrictions are arguably permissible under current doctrine.

Restrictions on *place* that preclude access to symbolic settings can be similarly distorting. As law professor Timothy Zick has noted, "Speakers like abortion clinic sidewalk counselors, petition gatherers, solicitors, and beggars seek the critical expressive benefits of proximity and immediacy." Zick observes that current doctrine means "individuals who wish to engage in speech, assembly, and petition activities are too often displaced by a variety of regulatory mechanisms, including the construction of 'speech zones.'" Take, for example, a labor protest. A strike that occurs in front of an employer's business rather than blocks or miles away not only communicates to a different audience but also conveys different meanings.[15]

Restrictions on *manner* can drain an expressive message of its emotive content. A ban on singing could weaken the significance of a civil rights march, a funeral procession, or a memorial celebration. Manner restrictions can also eliminate certain classes of people from the forum altogether. That might be true of a requirement that all expression be conveyed by handbills or leaflets rather than by posters. As Supreme Court Justice William Brennan once observed, "The average cost of communicating by handbill is . . . likely to be far higher than the average cost of communicating by poster. For that reason, signs posted on public property are doubtless 'essential to the poorly financed causes of little people.'"[16]

Under current doctrine, the state's regulation of public spaces through time, place, and manner restrictions is too easily justified apart from serious inquiry into the implications of those restrictions. A government official can usually come up with some reason to regulate expressive activity, some explanation of neutrality, and some argument that an ample alternative for communication exists. But the First Amendment should require more than just any justification to overcome its presumptive constraint against government action.[17]

Sometimes the government can go to even greater extremes than the latitude afforded under time, place, and manner restrictions. Under an evolving doctrine known as *government speech*, the government can characterize some expression as distinctively its own and not subject to *any* First Amendment review.

Not all applications of the government speech doctrine are problematic; some cases are easy to understand. When the City of Pawnee hosts a tribute to black history on Martin Luther King Jr. Day, it is "speaking" a message consistent with Dr. King's values. To that end, it need not ensure that members of the Ku Klux Klan have an opportunity to present their perspective. The event is premised on government speech rather than on facilitating a diversity of viewpoints and ideas.

Even though we can readily grasp the easy cases, the government speech doctrine is fiercely contested by courts and legal scholars because the line drawing it requires beyond those easy cases is impossible to configure. And without any lines—if the government could claim its own speech in any possible forum—the doctrine would swallow the First Amendment.

The Supreme Court unwisely gestured toward the possibility of an unrestricted government speech doctrine in its 2009 decision *Pleasant Grove v. Summum*. In that case, an obscure religious group called Summum wanted to erect a stone monument in a city park in Pleasant Grove City, Utah. Summum argued that because Pleasant Grove's park was a traditional public forum, the city could not limit the privately donated monuments in the park to those representing certain mainstream groups, like a statue of the Ten Commandments. The city responded that the park space was a limited resource that could only accommodate a limited number of monuments, and insisted that it could choose which ones to include. In some ways the city's argument makes sense—public parks are finite resources and cannot possibly accommodate every monument that every person wanted to contribute. But rather than addressing that issue within a public forum analysis, the Supreme Court ducked the issue by designating the monuments in the city park as government speech. That meant Pleasant Grove could decide which monuments to allow and which ones to prohibit. Sidestepping the public forum analysis avoided the hard work that courts and officials should be required to undertake in these settings.[18]

PROPER LIMITS

The preceding critiques do not mean that governmental actors are without any recourse when they want to regulate the public forum. When Pawnee hosts a forum on a local government shutdown, Leslie Knope rightly silences a participant who asks, "With the government shut down, who's going to stop Al Qaeda?" That kind of question, while legitimately of public concern, has no plausible relevance to a forum in Pawnee. In other words, governmental actors can appropriately limit a forum to particular issues and require that discussion focus on those issues. Additionally, some forums can be limited to certain classes of people. For example, it makes sense that public universities can limit student groups to students.[19]

Limitations on the public forum might also be permissible when they respond to exigent circumstances or are narrowly tailored to ensure public safety or access to public spaces. The most obvious example is that governmental actors can prevent expression in a public forum that threatens imminent violence. Other restrictions might also make sense. For example, a municipality might limit protests on public streets on mornings when street cleaning occurs. Firefighters could disperse a peaceful gathering if necessary to reach a burning building. And as the Supreme Court has emphasized, "governmental authorities have the duty and responsibility to keep their streets open and available for movement." For this reason, "a group of demonstrators could not insist upon the right to cordon off a street, or entrance to a public or private building, and allow no one to pass who did not agree to listen to their exhortations."[20]

The limitations on the public forum are important. We may rightly worry when expression in a public forum risks violence or disrupts important means of access. But government's willingness to endure potentially disruptive or harmful expression in the public forum ought to be exceedingly high. Otherwise, we risk marginalizing or eliminating meaningful access to government-provided places for engagement across difference.

THE PRIVATE PUBLIC FORUM

What happens when public forums are replaced by forums owned and managed by private actors rather than by the government? The use of privately owned spaces for public discussion long predates the judicial recognition of the public forum in the mid-twentieth century. One of the most common examples of these spaces is the public house. We know it today by its shorthand: the pub. The roots of the pub are traceable to early Rome, but they gained a foothold with taverns in British culture, including in the American colonies. Food activist and lawyer Baylen Linnekin observes that colonial taverns were used "for nearly every public purpose, including 'council and assembly meetings, social gatherings, merchants' associations, preaching, [and] the acting of plays.'" Historian Peter Thompson argues that the "speech and action" that emerged from these places "were shaped by an awareness of the tavern as public space."[21]

Most of today's taverns and pubs lack the historical and cultural significance of those in colonial times, but they remain important examples of private spaces that facilitate public discourse and civic life. One of them is the Three Kings Public House, a cozy establishment a few blocks away from my house in St. Louis. Three Kings has a great happy hour and a fantastic selection of draft beers. I have attended planning meetings, philosophy seminars, theological debates, counseling sessions, writing groups, and birthday celebrations there. I have overheard brilliance and nonsense at the tables around me (and sometimes a little of both at my own table). Public discourse and civic life unfold at Three Kings.

Our popular imagination is filled with other examples of bars, coffee shops, and diners that serve similar roles: Cheers is the Boston bar "where everybody knows your name." Central Perk was the gathering place for Monica, Rachel, and the rest of the Friends. Local diners figure prominently in shows like *Seinfeld*, *Saved by the Bell*, and *Friday Night Lights*. Those gathering places also extend to the real world. The Stonewall Inn served as a hub of early gay rights activism that culminated in the 1969 Stonewall riots. The Amazingrace coffeehouse grew out of antiwar protests at Northwestern University during the 1970s. More recently, protesters, organizers, and journalists in Ferguson, Missouri, found an informal meeting place in MoKaBe's Coffeehouse.[22]

Today's private public forums aren't limited to where we eat. We also gather in privately owned shopping malls, streets, and parks. One of the most prominent examples in recent years is Zuccotti Park, the privately owned park in Lower Manhattan that became the focal point of the Occupy Wall Street protest in 2011. The park, originally (and not without some irony) named Liberty Plaza Park, took shape during a strange season of horse trading in the 1960s between city planners and real estate developers that gave the latter zoning variances in exchange for the public use of their private spaces. New York City has more than 500 of these private parks, and they provide 3.5 million square feet of space for public use. Curiously, while city-owned parks have curfews, the original zoning rules for these privately owned public spaces require that they remain open twenty-four hours a day. This odd legal arrangement made the private public forums more attractive to Occupy than the real public forums—one can't create a tent city in a location subject to a curfew.[23]

And so the Occupiers came to Zuccotti Park. Beginning in September 2011, they set up campgrounds and staging areas. They camped for 59 days, and the owners of the park sued to evict them. The owners prevailed, and police and protesters clashed sporadically in the weeks that followed. And all of the pitfalls and the promises of the symbolic anchor of the Occupy Movement unfolded in one of these strange but increasingly important private public forums.[24]

The growing prominence of private public forums raises a tension within our current understanding of the public forum. On the one hand, we value ownership and control of private property. On the other hand, we recognize the importance of common spaces to the discourse that enacts our First Amendment aspirations, even when those spaces are privately owned. And we know that private actors can coercively constrain discourse. For example, my colleague Gregory Magarian has documented how shopping malls in cities with patriotic or military communities threw out citizens protesting the Iraq War. Professor Magarian observes that these examples remind us that government is not alone in its "capacity to coerce behavior and impede personal freedom."[25]

The Supreme Court has examined some of these questions in the context of privately owned shopping centers, though its position has been far from clear. In 1968 the Court concluded that a private shopping center open to the public could not prevent citizens from exercising their First Amendment rights on its property. Justice Hugo Black, writing in dissent, suggested that the relevant question was "Under what circumstances can private property be treated as though it were public?" Four years later, the Court went a different direction in upholding the right of a shopping center to exclude Vietnam War protesters who had wanted to distribute handbills. Then, in 1980, the Court clarified that individual states could still impose restrictions on private shopping centers in order to protect the expressive liberties of patrons and visitors.[26]

We have not heard anything more from the Court on this issue, and Justice Black's question remains largely unanswered. But private public forums remain a significant part of our social and economic lives. They include the 48,000 shopping centers across the United States, with a combined 6 billion square feet of retail space. The millions of people setting foot in those places find few expressive liberties in the winding pathways that connect Banana Republic to Auntie Anne's Pretzels.[27]

Our social and economic interactions in shopping centers are increasingly outpaced by online commerce sites like Amazon and online social networks like Facebook. And our online interactions occur almost entirely on privately owned networks and Internet service providers (ISPs). Law professor Mark Lemley has observed that "public accessibility of [the Internet's] key features is so deeply ingrained that we simply take it for granted." But most private providers enforce terms of service through which they exercise significant discretion to censor expression or terminate service altogether. The more we migrate our communications and interactions online, the more we channel them into private public forums. In some ways, ISPs and social networks like Facebook are the shopping malls, cable television companies, and newspapers of old—privately run businesses whose services place them at the nexus of our social, political, and economic interactions.[28]

Online private public forums raise a host of unresolved legal questions that further complicate the public forum doctrine. Consider the challenge of *nesting*—when a forum or group in one legal category falls within a larger forum of a different category. For example, a government agency might host a policy discussion (creating a limited public forum) on Facebook (a private public forum). Law professor Lyrissa Lidsky notes that in these situations "it is not clear into what First Amendment category an interactive government sponsored social media site falls" or how we should balance the editorial discretion of the government officials running the online discussion with any monitoring or filtering that Facebook might impose.[29]

Twitter provides another example. The Nation of Islam's Twitter handle, @OfficialNOI, boasts over 12,000 followers. As a voluntary group, the Nation of Islam "maintains rules such as a ban on interracial dating, a dress code for women (including head coverings and no makeup or tight clothing) and a focus on traditional gender roles within the family." It also has the legal right to deny women access to some of its meetings. Twitter, in contrast, is a commercial entity subject to a host of regulations that prevent it from adopting similar rules: it could not deny its services to women or interracial couples, and it could not require its female employees to wear head coverings.[30]

The online nesting of the Nation of Islam within Twitter's social network raises important questions of control. Should Twitter as a commercial entity be allowed to promote and foster groups whose norms it is forbidden from promoting and fostering? Conversely, is Twitter the kind of private public forum with enough market share to warrant some limits on how it treats groups that do not conform to its own norms—might we have reasons to prevent Twitter from denying an account to the Nation of Islam? Offline, we have surprisingly few examples of voluntary groups nested within private public forums. But online social networks create millions of these relationships. And that gives online private public forums extraordinary power—arguably more power than that exerted by the shopping malls of an earlier generation.[31]

Confident pluralism depends upon meaningful venues for people to voice dissent and difference and to participate in dialogue across difference. As law professor Dawn Nunziato has argued, public forums "subsidize the speech of those who otherwise would not be able to express themselves effectively." They are part of "the government's affirmative obligations under the First Amendment to establish and protect the pre-conditions of democratic self-government." The more ubiquitous private public forums become—online and offline—the more courts will need to ensure that similar possibilities are preserved in some privately owned spaces.[32]

The extent to which private public forums should be constitutionally required to serve roles akin to traditional public forums ought to depend on a number of factors like market share, proximity to public spaces, and the significance of the discourse. These conceptual challenges are not entirely unprecedented. Writing almost a half-century ago, and addressing a different set of technological innovations, legal scholar Jerome Barron warned of "nongoverning minorities" that controlled access to the flow of information. Powerful media corporations, Barron contended, had developed that "an antipathy to ideas" that required "legal intervention if novel and unpopular ideas are to be assured a forum" because "unorthodox points of view which have no claim on broadcast time and newspaper space as a matter of right are in a poor position to compete with those aired as a matter of grace."[33]

In the context of today's private public forums, we might consider more carefully the ways in which unorthodox views confront the risk of being excluded from important social and communications networks. We might also pay greater attention to the meaning of "ample alternatives of communication." That inquiry will necessarily be context-specific, but it might help focus our attention on those settings in which private public forums have effectively foreclosed alternatives for communication.

THE LIMITS OF THE PRIVATE PUBLIC FORUM

As we consider the looming challenges of the private public forum, it is important to recognize some limiting principles. Not every space where discourse happens is a public forum. Pubs and shopping malls raise important borderline questions, but other venues do not. My friends and I may engage in extensive public discourse at my house, but that does not make my house anything close to a public forum.

Most judges and lawyers would agree about my house. But the consensus breaks down rather quickly when we move beyond private residences. Consider, for example, the prohibition of discrimination in places of "public accommodation," which gained prominence under Title II of the Civil Rights Act of 1964. The original federal legislation encompassed inns, restaurants, gas stations, and places of entertainment but exempted private clubs and other establishments "not in fact open to the public." Some state public accommodations laws now extend to all commercial businesses. And some courts have carelessly concluded that *groups* like the Boy Scouts are *places* of public accommodation. That logic undercuts the purpose of public accommodations laws. It also distracts us from focusing on the kinds of private public forums that actually function as proxies for public forums in their facilitation of public discourse. Internet service providers fill this role; in most cases, private membership organizations like the Boy Scouts do not.[34]

THE PUBLIC FORUM REQUIREMENT

Season 4 of *Parks & Recreation* finds Leslie Knope tussling with her boss, Ron Swanson, about Ron's boys-only group, the Pawnee Rangers. Leslie forms her own girls-only group, and conflict erupts when the two groups camp near each other. In the midst of shouting and disagreement about the merits of single-sex groups, one of the girls asks Leslie: "What about a public forum? You always say that there's no better solution for a hot-button issue than a good old-fashioned public forum."[35]

We need more "good old-fashioned public forums." We need limited public forums to work through specific issues and disagreements. But we also need public forums to facilitate our voicing and venting of ideas and emotions: traditional forums like streets, sidewalks, and parks; forums like those hosting student organizations on public college and university campuses; and virtual forums like Internet service providers and social networking sites.

Toward these ends, the public forum requirement suggests the following principle:

> Government should honor its commitment to ensure public forums for the voicing of dissent and discontent. Expressive restrictions in these forums should only be justified by compelling

government interests. Private public forums that effectively supplant these government-sponsored forums should in some cases be held to similar standards.

The public forum requirement that I have formulated does not reflect current legal doctrine. But something like it is not wholly unfamiliar to our own history and tradition. Writing during the heart of the civil rights era, law professor Harry Kalven took aim at two of the Supreme Court's then-recent decisions pertaining to civil rights protests in public places. Kalven noted that the opinions "bristled with cautions and with a lack of sympathy for such forms of protest." He insisted that "the generosity and empathy with which [public forums] are made available is an index of freedom."[36]

The public forum requirement secures the places and spaces for the enactment of confident pluralism across difference. These legal protections do not guarantee that confident pluralism will actually unfold in public forums—those responsibilities fall on us and our civic practices (the subject of the second half of the book). Nor will the public forum resolve all of our disagreements—the real world does not have a sitcom ending. But it remains an integral part of confident pluralism—the space where we come together to work on our discourse and our civic life.

CHAPTER 4

THE PUBLIC FUNDING REQUIREMENT

TAX EXEMPTIONS, STUDENT FORUMS, AND GOVERNMENT ORTHODOXIES

By the end of this chapter, I hope to have convinced you that (1) the public forum principles discussed in the previous chapter extend to some forms of funding, including the funding that flows from charitable tax-exempt status under the Internal Revenue Code, and (2) these principles extend even to those groups that we most detest—even, most famously, to a racially discriminatory private school like Bob Jones University. I will begin with a more sympathetic example. But I will ultimately argue that *today* (and the historical and contextual qualifiers are important), a modern-day Bob Jones should be eligible for tax-exempt status. I am aware that the claim is controversial. As the child of an interracial marriage, I will be arguing that the principles of the public forum should extend to an organization whose policies reject the viability of my very existence.[1]

FUNDING THE PUBLIC FORUM

If you have felt a bit of whiplash moving from *facilitating* to *funding*—from Leslie Knope to Bob Jones University—you are not alone. But it turns out that the concepts are more related than they first appear. When the Pawnee Parks & Recreation Department hosts a public forum, Pawnee tax dollars pay for Leslie Knope and her colleagues to prepare for the forum, to arrive early to set up chairs and make sure the microphones work, and to lead the discussion during the forum. Pawnee tax dollars pay for the building, the chairs, the lighting, and the sound system. All across America, in the real Pawnees, and in cities much larger, real Leslie Knopes spend real time and real dollars to host public forums. In other words, the public forum does not appear out of nowhere, with free meeting space for the forum and free electricity to keep the lights on. Government dollars pay for the spaces, the utilities, and the employees who make public forums possible. Facilitating pluralism means funding pluralism.[2]

Another reason to pay careful attention to the question of public funding is the ubiquity of government dollars in today's regulatory state. Not every government funding decision is constitutionally problematic or in tension with confident pluralism. But we might be especially concerned when government constrains *generally available* funding in settings that welcome and encourage a diversity of viewpoints and ideas.

One example of generally available funding comes through the tax-exempt status available to charitable, educational, and religious organizations under the Internal Revenue Code. The "coming together" enabled by the incentive structure of a tax deduction does not always involve a literal conversation or exchange of ideas. But the expressiveness, the politics, and the practices facilitated by a monetary contribution to a tax-exempt group are almost always dependent upon people acting in concert with one another. Tax-exempt organizations are not individual ventures but are cobbled together and sustained by people who identify with something larger than themselves.[3]

THE FEDERAL TAX DEDUCTION

The federal tax code effectively allows individual taxpayers to direct federal dollars to charitable, religious, and educational nonprofits of their choosing. Each qualifying deduction claimed by taxpayers provides something like an indirect government subsidy to the organization receiving the donation. A taxpayer who itemizes her deductions sees her tax liability reduced by an amount equal to her donation multiplied by her income tax rate.[4]

By way of example, suppose that Sally donates $100 to the Girl
Scouts and itemizes her deduction on her federal income taxes.
Suppose further that her income is taxed by the federal government at a 30 percent rate. Under section 170(c) of the Internal Revenue Code, and because the Girl Scouts are a tax-exempt organization under section 501(c)(3), Sally pays $30 less in taxes based on
her $100 donation. She is only out-of-pocket $70 for the $100 that
the Girl Scouts received. That means, in effect, that the government
has paid—or, we might say, subsidized—$30 of Sally's $100 donation.

In fact, the Supreme Court has on multiple occasions equated
the benefits of tax-exempt status to a financial subsidy. But while
Sally's forgone tax revenue can be viewed as an indirect government subsidy of the Girl Scouts, the selected organization and the
amount of the subsidy come at her discretion. Under this approach,
organizations and ideas wither or thrive not by government fiat, but
rather based on what law professors John Colombo and Mark Hall
have called the "values and the choices of private givers."[5]

Whatever its original purpose, the federal tax code now sup-
ports this pluralistic endeavor for an expansive range of groups.
The meanings of "charitable" and "educational" under the Internal Revenue Code are deliberately broad, and "religious" organizations are not even defined. Together, these three categories of
tax-exempt organizations encompass a vast array of groups in civil
society. So vast that we could make a nice parlor game out of identifying the sheer variety of groups that qualify as charitable under
the code.

When I played that game, I discovered the Order of the Azure
Rose ("a Medieval/Renaissance re-creation Guild that portrays
an anachronistic Royal Court and Order of Chivalry"), the Critter
Connection ("a non-profit group dedicated to the rescue and reha-
bilitation of abandoned and neglected guinea pigs"), the Mormon
Transhumanist Association ("an international nonprofit organization that promotes radical flourishing in compassion and creation
through technology and religion"), Tall Clubs International ("a social organization for tall adults . . . to promote tall awareness among

tall men and women, and in the community"), the Immortality In-stitute ("an international, not-for-profit, membership-based orga-nization [whose] mission is 'to conquer the blight of involuntary death'"), and the American Cheese Education Foundation ("sup-port[ing] existing and new educational efforts to further educa-tional opportunities for all those interested in producing, market-ing, selling, and appreciating North America's artisan, farmstead, and specialty cheeses"). Each of these groups is a recognized chari-table organization under the federal tax code. And each of these groups is important and meaningful to the people who run them and the people who support them.[6]

Within the vast domain of groups that qualify as tax exempt, every one of us could find not only groups that we think belong, but also groups that we find harmful to society. And, of course, our lists of reprehensible groups would differ. The pro-choice group and the pro-life group, religious groups of all stripes (or no stripe), hunting organizations and animal rights groups—the tax deductions bene-fit them all. The resulting mosaic is neither thematic nor tidy, but it is in at least one sense beautiful: it enacts the aspirations of confi-dent pluralism. And it does so with government dollars.[7]

GENERALLY AVAILABLE FUNDING

It is helpful in the present discussion to distinguish between gen-erally available government funding and discretionary funding like contracts or grants. The federal tax code's recognition of deduc-tions for contributions made to charitable, religious, and educa-tional organizations falls within the former category. That is why, for example, withholding federal grants or contracts to Planned Parenthood for abortion-related services (which is currently re-quired under a federal law called the Hyde Amendment) does not lead inexorably to the conclusion that the government could yank Planned Parenthood's tax exemption. In both of these cases, the government would be making a spending decision about its money and a normative judgment about the viewpoint of an organization. But there is a conceptual difference between conditioning the award of discretionary grants and contracts on the one hand, and precluding access to a forum whose purpose or function is to facilitate a diversity of viewpoints and ideas.[8]

The importance of ensuring generally available funding within a public forum is best illustrated by *Rosenberger v. University of Virginia*, a 1995 Supreme Court decision involving student organizations at a public university. The university provided funding for student-run publications but withheld funds to one of them on the basis that it "primarily promotes or manifests a particular belief in or about a deity or an ultimate reality." The Supreme Court rejected this approach after concluding "the University does not itself speak or subsidize transmittal of a message it favors but instead expends funds to encourage a diversity of views from private speakers."[9]

The Court's observation about the nature of the university's funding scheme can also be applied to the government's recognition of the federal tax exemption. That is one reason that arguments about government "complicity" in these situations are misplaced. Consider the claim by political theorist Corey Brettschneider that the government risks appearing "neutral or indifferent to the content of viewpoints" of organizations that it subsidizes through generally available funding. Brettschneider expresses concern that this risk of misperception will make the government complicit in "protecting the views of liberal democracy's own opponents." He seems to extend this reasoning to tax exemptions, arguing that exemptions should only be available to groups that do not "seek to undermine the values of free and equal citizenship."[10]

There is little practical concern that tax-exempt status conveys any kind of government endorsement. The same is true for generally open forums like the forum for student groups at the University of Virginia. When the government offers these generally available resources, it should extend them to diverse viewpoints and ideas.

The government could, in some circumstances, close a forum altogether. In the context of the federal tax deduction, it could eliminate the generally available resource and then reallocate the money saved to discretionary grants and contracts for groups that endorse its normative commitments. That fiscal maneuvering might allow the government to realize the full potential of the government speech doctrine in the context of its spending decisions. It would be unwise from the perspective of confident pluralism, but it would at least have the virtue of coherence. More pragmatically, such a drastic reordering of public funding would encounter fierce resistance in the political process. And these political hurdles make sense: most of us do not want the government to have complete discretion in all of its spending decisions, and we think that the benefits of tax deductions are worth the costs. That is the lesson from a memorably named 1970s feminist magazine: *Big Mama Rag*.

BIG MAMA RAG

Big Mama Rag (or *Big Mama*, as it was called by its founders) published its first issue in October 1972. On the first page, a handwritten note announced: "Our hope is that the feelings expressed through *Big Mama Rag* will relate to the feelings of all women everywhere." The progressive magazine included short essays, news stories, book reviews, and poems. It drew upon feminist writers and thinkers ranging from Congresswoman Pat Schroeder to (the pre-celebrity) Roseanne Barr. And its broader intentions were clear from the start: "to serve as an effective communication system for surrounding area groups, actions and events." *Big Mama* was not just a magazine—it was a movement.[11]

Big Mama's obstacles were also clear from the beginning. The inaugural issue noted that getting started had been "quite a struggle" and that the founders were "in desperate need of more help." But the magazine prioritized its pulpit above its profits: "over two-thirds of each issue are distributed free, many to prisons and those hospitalized in mental institutions."[12]

After the first five issues, *Big Mama* took a more professional turn. The April 1974 issue had noticeably better typesetting. A new masthead replaced the initial list of handwritten names and added a note that the magazine was published by "a nonprofit corporation." But as the operation grew, so did expenses. Linda Fowler's column in the September 1974 issue drew attention to the austere arrangements of the staff: "Five of us are now living collectively, sharing a painting job and a secretarial job and working almost full-time on [the magazine]. *Big Mama* pays one $250/month salary, which we also share. (We are house painters—if you know of any jobs we can bid on, please get in touch.)"[13]

In September 1974, *Big Mama* filed for tax-exempt status under section 501(c)(3) of the Internal Revenue Code. IRS officials repeatedly denied the request. In September 1976 they informed *Big Mama* that if the magazine "were advocating homosexuality or encouraging people to engage in homosexual activity they would be barred from exemption as not educating the public on subjects useful to the public."[14]

Big Mama had never tried to hide its views. Its inaugural issue had contained an article titled "What Does the Word Lesbian Do to You?" The magazine had designated the Oct/Nov 1973 issue as the "Lesbian/Feminist Issue," which included a range of articles on lesbianism and a series of letters collected under the heading "Ask a Lez." Most subsequent issues contained multiple lesbian-focused articles, letters, and advertisements.[15]

The November 1976 issue highlighted the tangible financial consequences that came from the IRS's denial: "Besides the legal issue involved, the granting of tax exempt status would have immediate economic implications for *Big Mama*. The newspaper would become eligible for the Post Office's much cheaper non-profit rates." The column also noted the palpable strain of the bureaucratic battle: "[*Big Mama*] has been turned down repeatedly, first at the local level, then at progressively higher levels of the IRS."[16]

Big Mama sued the IRS the following year. After a loss in federal district court, the magazine appealed. Its brief emphasized that it was "heavily dependent upon charitable donations for its support" and that a few years earlier "over 50 percent of its income consisted of charitable contributions, grants or funds raised through benefits."[17]

Big Mama viewed tax-exempt status as crucial to its ongoing mission: "the organization's sole purpose in seeking tax-exempt status under I.R.C. § 501(c)(3) is to enable it to be eligible for tax-deductible contributions." The magazine's "hand-to-mouth existence" was "dependent on donations from private individuals and organizations." Critically, *Big Mama* also drew attention to the broad meanings of "educational" and "charitable" under the Internal Revenue Code:

> This is why, for example, the operation of an automobile drag strip has been held to be "for either charitable or educational purposes." This is also why the production of an annual football "bowl" game and halftime show has been held to be educational. And this is why the IRS itself has issued countless revenue rulings which recognize that the terms "charitable" and "educational" accommodate activities as wide ranging as dancing, selling toys, sailboat racing, group harmony singing, and many more.[18]

In September 1980, the appellate court rejected the IRS's "discriminatory denial of tax exemptions." *Big Mama*'s issue the following month brought a cautiously optimistic report, noting that "the importance of tax-exempt status" was that "the project is heavily reliant upon charitable contributions for our continued existence."[19]

But even the legal victory left unresolved challenges: "winning a federal tax-exempt number doesn't give you exemption for federal excise tax and you still have to get a state tax exempt status." Those other battles continued. In April 1984 *Big Mama* published these words: "Last issue, we're hoping to come back. . . ."[20]

They never did.

It is of course impossible to know whether an initial grant of tax-exempt status would have meant that *Big Mama* would still be around today, or even that it would have lasted longer than its twelve-year run. But it is worth noting that even after the ultimate victory in the courts, *Big Mama*'s editors remained circumspect: "We did win the case, but it took forever (8 years)." Eight years without a tax exemption. Eight years of costly and demoralizing bureaucratic handwringing, setbacks, and litigation. Eight years without the benefit of confident pluralism.

A TOUGHER CASE: BOB JONES UNIVERSITY

The story of *Big Mama Rag* and the nature of the Internal Revenue Code's charitable, educational, and religious deductions call to mind a more well-known denial of tax-exempt status involving the fundamentalist Christian school, Bob Jones University. The South Carolina school believed that interracial relationships were contrary to the Bible. Its particular concern was blacks marrying whites, but its policy restricted interracial dating of any kind:

There is to be no interracial dating.

1. Students who are partners in an interracial marriage will be expelled.
2. Students who are members of or affiliated with any group or organization which holds as one of its goals or advocates interracial marriage will be expelled.
3. Students who date outside their own race will be expelled.
4. Students who espouse, promote, or encourage others to violate the University's dating rules and regulations will be expelled.[21]

In 1971 the IRS issued a revenue ruling that declared "a school not having a racially nondiscriminatory policy as to students . . . does not qualify as an organization exempt from Federal income tax." Shortly thereafter, the IRS denied an exemption to a number of racially discriminatory religious schools, including Bob Jones in South Carolina and Goldsboro Christian Schools in North Carolina. Both schools challenged the application of the revenue ruling, and the case reached the Supreme Court.[22]

The schools lost 8 to 1. Chief Justice Warren Burger's opinion for the majority pronounced that an "institution's purpose must not be so at odds with the common community conscience as to undermine any public benefit that might otherwise be conferred." Burger concluded that "racial discrimination in education is contrary to public policy." The *New York Times* ran the headline: "Tax-Exempt Hate, Undone." The *Washington Post* raved that Bob Jones had been "trounced" at the Court. Despite popular reaction to the decision, commentators warned "it is a mistake to think *Bob Jones* an easy case."[23]

In fact, *Bob Jones*, while normatively attractive to almost everyone, is conceptually wrong. To be sure, the charitable deduction (and the law of charitable trust that preceded it) has always included a vague notion of "public benefit," which largely means that you cannot establish a charity for your own personal benefit. But that limitation is a long way from the notion of "common community conscience" asserted in *Bob Jones*. Justice Lewis Powell noted as much in his *Bob Jones* concurrence: "Far from representing an effort to reinforce any perceived 'common community conscience,' the provision of tax exemptions to nonprofit groups is one indispensable means of limiting the influence of governmental orthodoxy on important areas of community life."[24]

Lawyers often distinguish between the holding of a decision—its direct legal consequences—and the reasoning underlying the holding. Despite my disagreement with the reasoning in *Bob Jones*, the holding seems justified given the extraordinary context in which it emerged. *Bob Jones* upheld the denial of tax-exempt status to schools that discriminated against African Americans. The decision came in 1983, within a generation of *Brown v. Board of Education*, and it reached segregationist academies that resisted integration. *Bob Jones*, in other words, is linked inextricably with the history and context of the civil rights movement. It came on the tail end of extraordinary legal and judicial measures to further equality of citizenship and equality of opportunity for African Americans.[25]

These unique circumstances have been recognized by a number of distinguished scholars. Law professor Eugene Volokh notes that *Bob Jones* "rested expressly on the discrimination's being race discrimination, and on its being in education" and observes that no other cases are "dealing with massive nationwide efforts to dismantle a deeply entrenched discriminatory system that had deprived millions of people of important economic opportunities [or] . . . groups that exert a pervasive influence on the entire educational process." Political theorist Jeff Spinner-Halev asserts similarly that "the *Bob Jones* case was a matter of invidious discrimination because of the time and place in which it took place. . . . This case emerges out of the 1960s, with the US Government's attempts to outlaw school segregation, and its worries about the common Southern response of establishing private schools in order to preserve de facto segregation." And writing just prior to the Court's *Bob Jones* decision, law professor Douglas Laycock argued that "when private schools drain off most of the whites in a school system, as has happened in some cities, they preclude any meaningful public school desegregation."[26]

The historical context of *Bob Jones* is also borne out by the practical limitations on its holding. The IRS has never expanded its "public policy" constraint beyond race-based discrimination. In fact, the actual constraint may even be more limited. In 2006 a private school in Hawaii that limited admission to students of Hawaiian ancestry faced an antidiscrimination challenge. A federal appellate court sided with the school: race-based discrimination not involving African Americans did not raise the same public policy concerns.[27]

I realize, of course, that the *Bob Jones* decision is in some circles akin to a sacred text, and that one is not supposed to question even the reasoning of certain canonical decisions. But the logic of *Bob Jones* is inconsistent with the public forum framing of the federal tax exemption. We cannot begin with the premise that the public forum is open to all groups and then start excluding those groups we don't like.

We might answer that concern by asserting that "race is different"—that it provides the one categorical exception to the public forum framing. Such a response is not implausible. But it leads to a series of objections: Is race always different? Why, for example, does racial discrimination violate "public purposes" but not gender discrimination, even though the Supreme Court has found both forms of discrimination to violate the Equal Protection Clause? And if the Internal Revenue Service could define this standard once, what prevents it from doing so again?[28]

These questions are not just academic exercises. In April 2015 the

United States Supreme Court heard oral arguments in *Obergefell v. Hodges*, the case addressing whether the denial of same-sex marriage by states violates the Constitution. One telling exchange unfolded between Justice Samuel Alito and Donald Verrilli, the solicitor general of the United States. Justice Alito asked: "Well, in the *Bob Jones* case, the Court held that a college was not entitled to tax-exempt status if it opposed interracial marriage or interracial dating. So would the same apply to a university or a college if it opposed same-sex marriage?" General Verrilli replied: "It's certainly going to be an issue." Within days of the Court's decision in *Obergefell*, *New York Times* columnist Mark Oppenheimer invoked *Bob Jones* to argue that the government should eliminate tax-exempt status from "organizations that dissent from settled public policy on matters of race or sexuality."[29]

Before we jump too quickly to "Bob Jones-ing" today's religious colleges and universities, we might think carefully about the distinct challenges posed by racial discrimination against blacks in the Jim Crow South. We might ask whether cases like *Bob Jones* responded to a social context and institutional power structures that uniquely justified certain legal interventions. Recognizing the historical context of *Bob Jones* does not mean that we are today a "postracial" society. The dismal state of our current educational system is a stark reminder that the end of legal segregation in public and private schools has left us far short of meaningfully realizing the inclusion premise. But today's greatest challenges to racial inequality do not stem from formal exclusionary policies like those at issue in *Bob Jones*. Moralistic invocations of *Bob Jones* may make us feel better about our so-called commitment to racial equality by ensuring that groups that no longer exist continue to feel our scorn. But meaningfully addressing the immense and ongoing challenges of race in this country will require far more of an actual commitment in other areas of law and policy.[30]

These ideas are not original to me. Writing in the *Harvard Law Review* shortly after the *Bob Jones* decision, law professor Robert Cover argued that if the government seeks to destroy an undesirable way of life, it had better make an unambiguous commitment to an overriding constitutional concern. He saw no such commitment in the *Bob Jones* decision—and our continued ambivalence toward racial equality in this country suggests that his indictment still stands. Absent such a commitment, Cover worried deeply about the government's actions toward Bob Jones University.[31]

Professor Cover was not insensitive to racial injustice—he spent three weeks in a Georgia jail for helping the voting rights campaign of the Student Non-Violent Coordinating Committee in the 1960s. But he recognized the government's action in *Bob Jones* for what it was: a frontal assault on a private institution through the exercise of "superior brute force." This case wasn't primarily about withholding a discretionary benefit or avoiding government complicity—it was an effort to weaken and perhaps even destroy Bob Jones University. As Supreme Court Justice John Paul Stevens noted in a related case, "if the granting of preferential tax treatment would 'encourage' private segregated schools to conduct their 'charitable' activities, it must follow that the withdrawal of the treatment would 'discourage' them, and hence promote the process of desegregation." For Stevens, "this causation analysis is nothing more than a restatement of elementary economics: when something becomes more expensive, less of it will be purchased." He concluded: "If racially discriminatory private schools lose the 'cash grants' that flow from the operation of the statutes, the education they provide will become more expensive and hence less of their services will be purchased."[32]

Cover's article drew attention to briefs filed in support of Bob Jones by religious groups like the Mennonites and the Amish who were not themselves racially discriminatory: "The principle that troubled these [groups] was the broad assertion that a mere 'public policy,' however admirable, could triumph in the face of a claim to the First Amendment's special shelter against the crisis of conscience." Harvard Law School dean Martha Minow has written that Cover worried about "the power and practice of a government that rules by displacing, suppressing, or exterminating values that run counter to its own." She notes that "Cover faced up to the fact that some of the particular visions and norms rejected by the state may themselves be at odds with his own notions of human equality and liberty."[33]

THE LOGIC OF GENERALLY AVAILABLE FUNDING

Confident pluralism does not allow us to exclude from generally available resources those groups that we don't like. That is good news for *Big Mama*, but it might also be good news for a modern-day *Bob Jones*. And it means that generally available resources like the benefits of tax-exempt status should extend to organizations like the Nation of Islam, the Catholic Church, and Wellesley College. The public funding requirement is:

> When the government offers generally available resources (financial and otherwise) to facilitate a diversity of viewpoints and ideas, it should not limit those resources based on its own orthodoxy.

The IRS should not limit tax-exempt status based on viewpoint or ideology. State tax exemptions modeled after the federal one should be governed by that same standard. As law professors John Colombo and Mark Hall have argued, the public policy constraint on tax exemption "relegate[s] it to merely another mechanism for the government to, in effect, make direct spending decisions by selecting which nonprofit activities confer a sufficient benefit to the community to deserve tax relief." Instead, the longstanding charitable exemption is best justified by allowing donors to determine which charities they will fund. In the words of Supreme Court Justice William Brennan, tax-exempt organizations contribute to "the diversity of association, viewpoint, and enterprise essential to a vigorous, pluralistic society." Unless we were to fundamentally restructure the charitable deduction, we are confronted with something akin to a limited public forum premised on promoting a wide range of viewpoints and ideas.[34]

A similar logic applies to the forum of student organizations on public college and university campuses. Think back to the *Christian Legal Society* decision, which denied a Christian group "official recognition" and access to the public forum at a public law school.

Official recognition also brought some generally available financial resources—roughly $250 in the case of the Christian group. But the public forum requirement suggests that the logic of *Christian Legal Society* is wrong even if a larger allocation of generally available funding had been at issue. Public colleges and universities that establish forums for student organizations must welcome student organizations without regard to viewpoint or ideology. That includes extending generally available funding to them.

The public funding requirement insists that generally available resources are made available to any student organization. That principle should protect Christian groups in the current political climate on progressive public school campuses. It should also protect atheist or LGBT groups on conservative public school campuses. The *Christian Legal Society* decision is out of step with these basic principles.[35]

The public funding requirement, alongside the public forum requirement and the voluntary groups requirement, comprise the constitutional commitments of confident pluralism. These are the structural arrangements that we need to make confident pluralism possible. But constitutional commitments alone will not suffice. We also need to pursue the civic practices of confident pluralism in our own lives. The second half of the book turns to these practices.

Part II

CIVIC PRACTICES

CHAPTER 5

CIVIC aspirations
TOLERANCE, HUMILITY, AND PATIENCE

"Move your guilt-ridden ass to Ferguson, or shut your pie-hole." The words appeared in my email inbox a few moments after an essay of mine had gone live on CNN's website. I had written the piece in response to the events in Ferguson, Missouri, following the killing of Michael Brown by Officer Darren Wilson. Brown's killing sparked mass protests that placed Ferguson in the national spotlight.[1]

My essay made two basic points. First, it noted that the actual community of Ferguson was fairly diverse along racial and class lines, contrary to most media characterizations. Second, it argued that whether we lived in Ferguson or not, all of us were in some ways connected to and responsible for the broader racial and class challenges that the tensions in Ferguson highlighted.[2]

Dave from Chicago had decided to share his thoughts about my essay. I never read online comments about anything I write, but a few people like Dave have figured out that it's harder for me to ignore a direct email. I gathered that Dave's note was probably a representative sample of some of the online comments on my essay. If you have ever scrolled through the comments after any controversial article, you will know that my guess was warranted.

Twitter and other forms of social media create similar hazards. I'm fairly new to Twitter, but even in these early days I have encountered plenty of nasty tweets from people I do not know. Others have it far worse.

There is a reason for the Internet adage known as Godwin's Law: "As an online discussion grows longer, the probability of a comparison involving Nazis or Hitler approaches 1." Social media gives us the opportunity to be insulted by just about anyone.[3]

Let's call this the Dave Principle, in honor of Chicago Dave: *Many people are dismissive or insulting of those with other viewpoints.*

The Dave Principle is alive and well, but the Internet poses an equally pernicious problem in the opposite direction: some of us self-select out of everything we don't want to hear. We close ourselves off to opposing views, we only read news coverage that confirms or amplifies our prior beliefs, and we limit ourselves to websites that reflect our political, cultural, and religious preferences. In short, the Internet for many of us becomes a huge echo chamber in which we only hear the voices that agree with us. Everything we think, write, or say goes largely unchallenged, and our ideas become self-reinforcing. Law professor Cass Sunstein calls it "enclave deliberation." It's how my own writing would look if I only shared drafts with my mom, who thinks that everything I write is gold.[4]

Let's call this the Sandy Principle, in honor of my mom: *Many people only listen to viewpoints with which they already agree.*

Much of the online world is governed by either the Dave Principle or the Sandy Principle. We encounter dismissive and insulting voices, or we confine ourselves to uncritical and self-reinforcing ones. These principles also extend to our offline interactions. We see the Dave Principle on shirts, bumperstickers, and coffee cups. It unfolds when protests meet counterprotests, or when passersby shout at demonstrators. We see the Sandy Principle in our cities, our neighborhoods, and our schools; sometimes it's reflected in where we eat and shop. We even have cultural symbols for some of these divides: Red states and Blue states, Fox News and MSNBC, Whole Foods and Chick-fil-A.[5]

Instead of shutting down or avoiding those with whom we disagree, confident pluralism suggests that we can and should allow space for meaningful difference and the opportunity for persuasion. But that vision will require more than reorienting our online comments and Twitter feeds. Rather, it requires enough of us to embrace civic practices to make a difference in how we treat each other.

CONFIDENT ASPIRATIONS

The civic practices of confident pluralism that I discuss in the next three chapters build upon three aspirations: *tolerance, humility*, and *patience*. These three words are not self-evidently confident. In fact, we might think of them as concessions that come from a *lack* of confidence. If we are uncertain about our own beliefs, we might hedge against them with an openness to other perspectives.

It might seem less obvious that we would pursue tolerance, humility, and patience in light of our firmly held convictions. But it is in fact the confidence in our own views in the midst of deep difference that allows us to engage charitably with others. Rather than lashing out at others or remaining in our own echo chambers, we can pursue dialogue and coexistence even when (and perhaps especially when) we believe that our views are in fact the better ones. As the philosopher John Stuart Mill argued, we should allow others the "complete liberty of contradicting and disproving our opinion" and "on no other terms can a being with human faculties have any rational assurance of being right."[6]

Even if we are not inclined to embrace these aspirations because of confidence in our own views, we might choose to do so for other reasons. Consider the words of Supreme Court Justice William Brennan that in our pluralistic society, "we must be willing to abide someone else's unfamiliar or even repellant practice because the same tolerant impulse protects our own idiosyncrasies."[7]

Mill and Brennan offer two different justifications for engaging with difference. Mill points us to the vulnerability that conviction allows; Brennan gives us a self-interested reason for welcoming a diversity of opinions. We could point to other arguments grounded in other justifications. We can decide to engage charitably without agreeing on the reasons for doing so. In other words, tolerance, humility, and patience function within confident pluralism as *aspirations*, not finely tuned philosophical concepts. We can set out an idea of how we might act, recognizing that for some, those actions will reflect deeply held commitments, and for others they may be little more than pragmatically justified concessions. But if enough of us embrace these aspirations, we may be able to sustain a consensus for confident pluralism, even as we draw from eclectic and blended antecedents. As the philosopher Charles Taylor has suggested, "we would agree on the norms while disagreeing on why they were the right norms, and we would be content to live in this consensus."[8]

To help unpack these aspirations, imagine two characters, Jerry and Larry. (I know these names sound like they came out of a webinar, but bear with me.) Jerry is a conservative moralist. He seeks "morality" along the lines of many conservative religious traditions: "morality" is the set of sometimes complex rules from a text or community that governs and constrains behavior, telling you what is right and what is wrong. Larry is a liberal progressive. He desires "autonomy" in the fashion of contemporary liberalism: "autonomy" is the freedom in most cases to make your own decisions apart from a text or community, to follow your own passions wherever they lead you. Jerry finds troubling the relaxed sexual norms of certain progressive groups. Larry finds troubling the traditional sexual norms of certain conservative groups. Jerry is a Christian and Larry is an atheist. They disagree strongly about matters of religion and sexuality.[9]

Let's assume that Jerry and Larry are both white, male, heterosexual, about the same age, and in roughly the same income bracket. In other words, their differences, though stark, would be even more complicated if we introduced other real-world factors that contribute to our real-world pluralism.

Most of us are not reducible to either Jerry or Larry. Most of us diverge from one or more of the stipulations in the previous paragraph. Most of us blend complex beliefs and values in nuanced and sometimes contradictory ways. And labels like "conservative moralist" and "liberal progressive" do not fully specify or even reach many of the issues that divide us. But Jerry and Larry nevertheless reflect something about our approaches to some of the most contested cultural issues today. For this reason, they will be helpful in exploring the three civic aspirations of confident pluralism.

TOLERANCE

Tolerance is the most important civic aspiration. It means a willingness to accept genuine difference, including profound moral disagreement. Achieving it is no easy task. As the philosopher Bernard Williams has observed, tolerance is most needed when people find others' beliefs or practices "deeply unacceptable" or "blasphemously, disastrously, obscenely wrong." The basic difficulty of tolerance, Williams notes, is that we need it "only for the intolerable."[10]

But tolerance does not require embracing all beliefs and viewpoints as good or right. The philosopher Edward Langerak reminds us that "toleration is derived from the Latin *tolero*, which primarily connotes the enduring of something." Heeding this connotation, "we should distinguish toleration from indifference, resignation, timidity, and approval." We should aspire not to an "anything goes," happy-go-lucky tolerance, but to a practical enduring for the sake of coexistence. Jerry and Larry are not going to agree with one another on every important issue—they hold views about the world that are fundamentally at odds with one another. Even if one of them wanted to embrace the other's views, he could not do so while fully retaining his own beliefs. The depth of their disagreement, and the fact of that disagreement, precludes anything like ultimate approval.[11]

Parsing the difference between tolerance and approval requires the hard work of distinguishing between people and ideas. We should not underestimate how difficult that work will be. Tolerance asks that Jerry treat Larry with respect. It doesn't mean he will respect Larry's ideas. Every one of us holds ideas that others find unpersuasive, inconsistent, or downright loopy. More pointedly, every one of us holds ideas that others find morally reprehensible. For this reason, the philosopher Simon Blackburn is right to warn against what he calls "respect creep": the circumstances in which "the request for minimal toleration turns into a demand for more substantial respect, such as fellow-feeling, or esteem, and finally deference and reverence." The depth of our convictions cannot support "respect creep" across all of our differences.[12]

The tolerance of confident pluralism does not impose the fiction that all ideas are equally valid or morally harmless. It does require respecting people, aiming for fair discussion, and allowing for the space to differ about serious matters. This kind of tolerance also allows for the expression of moral judgments about beliefs and practices. Most people who oppose a particular belief or action do not want to soften their objections. The gay rights advocate wants to apply social pressure to religious groups that exclude on the basis of sexual conduct. The anti-abortion activist wants to characterize the act of abortion as the unjustified killing of a human being. Confident pluralism allows space for these kinds of moral judgments. As I explain more fully in the next chapter, it differentiates between the inevitability of offending through judgments about beliefs or actions, and a stigmatizing of other people.

HUMILITY

Humility requires even greater self-reflection and self-discipline than tolerance. It leads Jerry and Larry to recognize that their own beliefs and intuitions rest upon tradition-dependent values that cannot be empirically proven or fully justified by forms of rationality external to those traditions. That does not mean Jerry or Larry must lack confidence in his own convictions. Humility is instead a reminder of the limits of translation, and the difficulty of proving our deeply held values to one another. Yet humility also recognizes that our human faculties are inherently limited—our ability to think, reason, and reflect is less than perfect, a limitation that leaves open the possibility that we are wrong. That is one reason that all of us, whether religious or not, live and act on a kind of faith. As theologian Lesslie Newbigin observes, "We are continually required to act on beliefs that are not demonstrably certain and to commit our lives to propositions that can be doubted."[13]

Humility is based on the limits of what we can *prove*, not on claims about what is *true*. For this reason, it should not be mistaken for relativism. Diana Eck, the founder of Harvard's Pluralism Project, rightly insists that pluralism "does not require us to leave our identities and our commitments behind." Humility leaves open the possibility that there is right and wrong and good and evil.[14]

Our beliefs can also be known. In fact, many of us know these beliefs even if we can't prove them, just as we know lots of things that we can't prove. We know what we ate for breakfast last week. We know that we are loved (and sometimes that we are not loved). This kind of knowledge also extends to our moral beliefs. We know that burning someone alive is bad. We know that helping a vulnerable child is good. Many of us are also certain about more contested moral beliefs. And many of us confidently hold these beliefs even though some people don't share them and others even reject them.

Humility can also facilitate understanding across difference. Our ability to recognize that not everyone will comprehend our own beliefs and values can help us enter into someone else's world through a greater attentiveness to listening. As Rabbi Jonathan Sacks counsels, we "must learn to listen and be prepared to be surprised by others. . . . We must even, at times, be ready to hear of their pain, humiliation and resentment and discover that their image of us is anything but our image of ourselves." Psychologist Jonathan Haidt suggests a pragmatic value to listening: "if you really want to change someone's mind on a moral or political matter, you'll need to see things from that person's angle as well as your own." Of course, as Haidt notes, this particular kind of humility comes with a risk: "if you do truly see it the other person's way—deeply and intuitively— you might even find your own mind opening in response."[15]

While Jerry might be concerned that humility points to relativism, Larry might worry that it sounds a little too "religious." But the humility of confident pluralism need not be grounded in a particular tradition. The philosopher Friedrich Nietzsche despised humility—he thought it a Christian virtue that had no place in an enlightened world. Yet many people who dislike the Christian understanding of humility nevertheless embrace the concept of "epistemic humility"—the idea that our lack of certainty in or proof about our views should lead us to a more humble posture in our engagement with others. In this sense, the aspiration of humility may be coherent even to those who remain critical of more traditional notions of humility. Both Jerry and Larry can recognize that their own convictions are rooted in a kind of faith.[16]

PATIENCE

Patience involves restraint, persistence, and endurance. Here it is important to recognize that Jerry and Larry both think they are *right* in a profoundly deep way. They structure much of their lives around their ethical commitments, and they often want their normative views to prevail on the rest of society. But confident pluralism acknowledges that dialogue and persuasion usually take time. Conversely, a lack of patience too often gives way to coercion and even to violence.

Many of us will need patience to get to know one another across our differences, to stumble toward dialogue across the awkward distance that separates us. Sometimes we will need patience to endure differences that will not be overcome. Patience also encourages efforts to listen, understand, and perhaps even to empathize. Those activities are not the same as accepting or embracing another view. In fact, it may turn out that patience leads us to a deeper realization of the evil or depravity of an opposing belief. But we can at least assume a posture that moves beyond caricatured dismissals of others before we even hear what they have to say.

Patience does not always mean passivity. In some cases, we will urge action when we confront what we believe to be evil and injustice in the world. But in most ordinary circumstances, patience counsels toward restraint, persistence, and endurance. Even though Jerry and Larry may detest one another's lifestyles and beliefs, patience asks them to endure one another's existence. And it holds open the possibility that such endurance can lead to greater understanding and empathy.

THE REAL JERRY AND LARRY

Jerry and Larry are real-world characters, in every sense of the word. Jerry Falwell, who died in 2007, was the Southern Baptist preacher and founder of the Moral Majority, a conservative Christian political organization that rose to prominence in the 1980s. Larry Flynt is the founder of *Hustler* magazine and an icon of the pornography industry.[17]

The real Jerry and the real Larry leave most of us uncomfortable. Larry once called on God to afflict a conservative news anchor "with a brain aneurysm that will lead to his slow and painful death." Jerry blamed the September 11, 2001, terrorist attacks on "the pagans and the abortionists and the feminists and the gays and the lesbians . . . the ACLU, People for the American Way—all of them who have tried to secularize America." Jerry and Larry have made plenty of other comments along these lines.[18]

The two men did not think much of each other. During the 1970s Jerry repeatedly condemned Larry's line of work. Larry said: "He called me every terrible name he could think of—names as bad, in my opinion, as any language used in my magazine." Larry eventually took offense. In 1983 he published a parody of Jerry using a then-famous advertisement for Campari liqueur. The actual advertisement relied on a double entendre that compared the "first time" a particular celebrity had tasted Campari to the celebrity's first sexual experience. In Larry's spoof, Jerry described his "first time" as being with his mother, while they were "drunk off our God-fearing asses." In the parody, Jerry explained that "Mom looked better than a Baptist whore with a $100 donation," and claimed he decided to have sex with her because she had "showed all the other guys in town such a good time." For good measure, Larry threw in a line about Jerry's preaching: "I always get sloshed before I go out to the pulpit. You don't think I could lay down all that bullshit *sober*, do you?"[19]

Larry's spoof led to a famous Supreme Court decision, which among other things, upheld Larry's right to publish the parody. The litigation proved contentious throughout. During his deposition, Jerry's lawyers asked Larry if his objective in the spoof had been to destroy or harm Jerry's character reputation. Larry, not one to mince words, relied, "To assassinate it." The facts and the law surrounding that decision are intriguing in their own right. But in unpacking the civic aspirations of confident pluralism, I am more interested in what this case tells us about the interaction between our civic practices and our constitutional commitments. Protecting the spoof was right because of, not in spite of, confident pluralism. Larry's initial decision was personal: whether he would extend tolerance, humility, and patience toward Jerry. By all accounts, Larry failed miserably (just as Jerry failed miserably in his prior dealings with Larry). But those civic failings shifted to constitutional questions when Larry's spoof became a lawsuit. At that point, the issue was not whether Larry would choose to embrace confident pluralism but whether the state would punish him for failing to do so. The right answer, though not without a cost, was to permit Larry to publish his spoof. Not all of our actions can or should be regulated by law. One of the paradoxes of confident pluralism is that its constitutional commitments must allow for its rejection in our civic practices. Nowhere is this more evident than in our speech.[20]

CHAPTER 6

LIVING SPEECH
RISING ABOVE INSULTS AND BULLYING

"Mom looked better than a Baptist whore with a $100 donation." Larry said some pretty nasty things about Jerry (and Jerry's mother). We can all think of even worse examples. When it comes to our speech, the First Amendment allows us to say almost anything to anyone.

Actually, that's not quite right. There are plenty of things we can't say. You can't tell a hit man, "I'll pay you $500 to kill my sister." You can't tell an investor (based on your insider knowledge), "I know for a fact that the stock price is going to drop at the opening bell tomorrow." You can't lie on the witness stand, unlawfully disclose classified information, or shout fire in a crowded theater (in the absence of reasonable belief that there is a fire).[1]

But when it comes to *offensive* speech, we have the liberty to say almost anything to anyone, even when our words injure the dignity and self-respect of other people. As the Supreme Court recently observed, "as a Nation we have chosen . . . to protect even hurtful speech on public issues to ensure that we do not stifle public debate." This assertion reflects longstanding First Amendment principles that "speech remains protected even when it may stir people to action, move them to tears, or inflict great pain." And so, when Larry defeated Jerry at the Supreme Court, the justices announced that speech may not be restricted even though it "may have an adverse emotional impact on the audience." Even more controversially, when a group of neo-Nazis dressed in Nazi attire and paraded down the street of a town filled with Holocaust survivors, the Illinois Supreme Court concluded: "We do not doubt that the sight of [the swastika] is abhorrent to the Jewish citizens of Skokie, and that the survivors of the Nazi persecutions, tormented by their recollections, may have strong feelings regarding its display. Yet it is entirely clear that this factor does not justify enjoining defendants' speech."[2]

FIRST AMENDMENT PERMISSIVENESS

The First Amendment makes it difficult for the government to regulate private expression that causes emotional, reputational, and psychological harm—expression like defamation and hate speech. Consider, for example, a famous free speech case from over seventy years ago, *Chaplinsky v. New Hampshire*. The Court noted that government officials could prohibit words "which by their very utterance inflict injury or tend to incite an immediate breach of the peace." Law professor Rodney Smolla has noted that this passage from *Chaplinsky* identifies two distinct reasons for restricting expression: (1) when it "inflicts injury"; and (2) when it "incites an immediate breach of the peace."[3]

The latter rationale, incitement to a breach of peace, reflects an outer limit on expression that remains in place today. But notice that this limit has nothing to do with the defamatory or hateful content of expression, or the harm that the expression actually inflicts upon the people it targets. In fact, because the constraint is based upon the threat of violence, those most likely to react violently are most protected from harmful speech while those least capable of violence are left exposed. We are left in the strange situation that would "permit a state to penalize a speaker who insults a burly construction worker while forbidding the punishment of the reviler of a wheelchair-bound" quadriplegic.[4]

The first prong of *Chaplinsky*—words that inflict injury— provides a separate rationale for limiting expression. As Professor Smolla notes, it suggests that some "words *by their very utterance* are deemed to inflict injury." At first blush, that makes sense. Some expression really does cause injury in its actual utterance. Most of us recognize this at a gut level. We've heard—or spoken—hurtful speech that can't simply be "taken back." At about the same age we learn that "sticks and stones can break my bones but words can never hurt me," most of us experience some words that actually do hurt.[5]

When it comes to this kind of hurtful speech, the solution of "counterspeech" won't do. It is not quite enough to say in the words of Supreme Court Justice Louis Brandeis, that "the fitting remedy for evil counsels is good ones." As literary scholar Stanley Fish has put it, the argument that harmful speech should be answered by more speech "would make sense only if the effects of speech could be canceled out by additional speech, only if the pain and humiliation caused by racial or religious epithets could be ameliorated by saying something like 'So's your old man.'"[6]

Even though we know that some offensive words will cause harm by their very utterance, those words can seldom be limited under the First Amendment. Indeed, outside of narrowly drawn tort limits on defamation and libel, one is hard pressed to find an example of a constitutionally permissible restriction of private expression linked only to emotional, psychological, or reputational injury. And even defamation and libel judgments are difficult to sustain when harmful words blur the line between fact and opinion.[7]

Our First Amendment permissiveness is not all bad. I would prefer it to a lot of alternatives. Indeed, the difficulty with the exceptions proves the value of the rule. Take the longstanding efforts to establish speech norms in workplaces and universities. As journalist Jonathan Rauch has observed, even though "hate speech" regulations are generally unconstitutional, "indirect, bureaucratic prohibitions have burrowed into workplaces and universities." By way of example, Rauch notes "federal law holds employers civilly liable for permitting the workplace to become a 'hostile environment'—a fuzzy concept which has been stretched to include, for example, a Bible verse printed on a paycheck (could upset an atheist) or a Seventh-day Adventist's discussion of religion ('religious harassment' because it 'depressed' a plaintiff)." The problem is even worse in many colleges and universities. Philosophy professor Timothy Shiell has summarized the conundrum: "[Hate speech] and the real-life cases it involves leave most people unsettled: they think that there are egregious cases that deserve sanctions, yet they also recognize that regulatory policies are often vague and can be arbitrarily or otherwise wrongly enforced."[8]

THE CHALLENGE FOR US

The freedom to say almost anything to anyone places a great deal of responsibility back on us: How should we think about our own speech? This question has no easy answers, and it confronts a culture that prides itself on free speech platitudes. Yet there remains for us the possibility of choosing what legal scholar James Boyd White has called *living speech*. As White observes, we can "seek to imagine speech in a worthy way—to distinguish what has real value as speech from that which is destructive of the value of speech."[9]

We could spend a lot of time discussing what we think "is destructive of the value of speech." We could have fierce debates over the role of obscene expression or commercial speech in public discourse. But for purposes of confident pluralism and the pursuit of tolerance, patience, and humility in our civic practices, we can identify two particularly destructive forms of speech: the hurtful insult and the conversation stopper. To understand each of these better, let's introduce a third character to join the conservative moralist and the liberal progressive: the bully.

We all know the bully. Some of us remember him—or her—from our own childhood. Some of us used to be the bully. As much as we would like to think otherwise, we also know the bully is not confined to the playgrounds and classrooms of our youth. He may get his start there, but he lives on in neighborhoods, schools, and online comments. He is alive and well in the workplace, in the university, and the halls of the legislature. The bully thrives off of the hurtful insult and the conversation stopper. Sometimes he enlists these devices to mask insecurity. Other times, he speaks out of an overconfidence that ignores tolerance, humility, and patience.

THE HURTFUL INSULT

One of the bully's most effective weapons is the hurtful insult. The bully often aims to *wound* with the hurtful insult—sometimes out of anger, other times out of his own wounds. The hurtful insult might be false, misleading, or hyperbolic—but it might also be true. It might be fact or opinion, or fall somewhere in between. It might be spoken out of humor, spite, or malice. The hurtful insult is almost impossible to regulate under the First Amendment.

Some versions of the hurtful insult, especially those based on race, gender, and sexuality, are not fit to print on the pages of this book. Others remain more commonplace but can sting just as much: *fat, ugly, stupid, friendless.* The hurtful insult often aims for the most vulnerable dimensions of our humanity.

The hurtful insult is *socially constructed.* It gains force and power by the cultural context that surrounds it. That also means that socially constructed hurtful insults can change over time. These changes in social meaning are too often dismissed by those worried about an overbearing "political correctness." To be sure, as I noted earlier, the enforcement of language norms on university campuses and elsewhere is an ongoing problem that rightly concerns free speech advocates. But an aversion to coercive enforcement of language norms should not distract us from recognizing the power and the harm of the hurtful insult.

One example of the socially constructed hurtful insult comes from the word "gay" in American English. The etymology of the word points to a number of different meanings, including "happy" and "lively." But most people today recognize that the word also refers to men who are sexually attracted to other men. This particular association led to a phrase that emerged in the 1980s: "that's so gay." At a time when social attitudes were far more hostile to same-sex attraction, the phrase usually served to link the connotation of male same-sex attraction to something that was either undesirable or effeminate.

It is increasingly clear that many uses of the phrase "that's so gay" are forms of the hurtful insult. For example, in a 2013 national survey of LGBT youth between the ages of thirteen and twenty-one, over half reported feeling unsafe at school because of their sexual orientation, and nearly three-quarters reported hearing the phrases "that's so gay" or "you're so gay" used in a negative way. While these kinds of phrases are unquestionably protected speech under the First Amendment, they are not invitations for discussion over contested values. They are cheap words that play on the social vulnerability of LGBT students.[10]

We should not dismiss these observations as political correctness gone awry. Rather, seeing the power—and the harm—of the hurtful insult can lead us toward a greater embrace of tolerance, humility, and patience. It can inform our choice of language for the sake of those around us.

THE CONVERSATION STOPPER

Sometimes the bully aims not to wound but to shut down conversation. We see the conversation stopper when the bully uses words like *close-minded, extremist, heretical,* and *militant.* These labels can be descriptive. They can also wound—their subjective effect on a person can cause deep hurt. More often than not, they are meant to end a conversation (not unlike "Shut your pie-hole"). As commentator Jonathan Chait intimates, the conversation stopper "makes debate irrelevant and frequently impossible." As with the hurtful insult, the conversation stopper cannot be restricted under the First Amendment.[11]

One of the most common examples of the conversation stopper today is the label of the "bigot." It frequently appears against religious believers and groups that maintain traditional beliefs about sexuality in their internal membership requirements. Kevin Cullen of the *Boston Globe* accuses Gordon College of a bigotry that "insults our intelligence" because the school's faith and conduct policy requires celibacy outside of heterosexual marriage. Hemant Mehnta calls a Tufts University policy that allows campus religious groups to select their leaders according to a similar policy "a religious exemption to bigotry." The bigotry rhetoric pervades Facebook pages, Twitter feeds, and online comments.[12]

To be sure, some religious believers *are* bigots: they "strongly and unfairly dislike other people" and they treat others with "hatred and intolerance." But the bigotry label is not generalizable to all religious believers who hold traditional beliefs about human sexuality, even when those beliefs lead to "discrimination" by private groups.[13]

To understand the limitations of the Bigot label, we might distinguish between *act* and *motive*. People don't like to be called "discriminators," and the label of "discrimination" often conveys a negative meaning. But the word has the merit of being descriptive: it usually connotes an expressive action rather than attributing a specific motive. Private religious groups with sexual conduct requirements discriminate against those who choose not to conform to those requirements. Selective colleges and universities like Vanderbilt discriminate against those who fail to meet their admissions criteria. Sports teams discriminate against untalented athletes. Wellesley College discriminates against men.

When Vanderbilt discriminates against an applicant with a low grade-point average, the resulting exclusion can be hurtful and stigmatizing. The same could be said of Wellesley's decision to exclude men or a religious group's decision to exclude on the basis of sexual conduct and belief. But these are not likely mean-spirited forms of exclusion. Indeed, it is plausible in each of these cases that the reasons for exclusion stem from the group's internal norms, beliefs, and goals.[14]

The bigot label, in contrast, attributes a particular motive to an action. And it does so with rhetorical force. We can debate whether some acts of discrimination are good or bad or simply neutral (like discriminating between two wines). But there are no good bigots.

Some of the people using the *bigot* label think that is exactly the point: there are no good bigots. From their perspective, *every* act of exclusion of gays and lesbians is a bigoted act, and therefore the label is morally appropriate. And this isn't the only example that comes to mind. The anti-abortion advocate who shouts "Baby Killer" at an abortion doctor believes that this is a descriptively accurate characterization. The religious believer who screams

"Heretic" is similarly convinced by the accuracy of the label. But it is not hard to see why these phrases are conversation stoppers.

Here's another one: just add "phobic" to something you care about, and you've got a ready-made conversation stopper against anyone who disagrees with you. The religious conservative who believes in traditional sexuality norms is "homophobic." The government official expressing concerns about Muslim terrorists is "Islamophobic." The school that hosts *The Vagina Monologues* is "transphobic." These are not arguments; they are conversation stoppers.[15]

THE POWER OF STIGMA AND THE
ROLE OF MORAL JUDGMENT

The hurtful insult and the conversation stopper can both stigmatize. Sociologist Erving Goffman hints at these connections in his powerful 1963 book, *Stigma: Notes on the Management of Spoiled Identity*. Goffman underscores the socially constructed nature of stigma, which depends on "a language of relationships, not attributes." The bully trades on these social understandings to cast people beyond the pale, either for who they are, or for what they believe (and often an inseparable combination of the two). The hurtful insult says: "I don't have to respect you as a human being." The conversation stopper says: "I don't have to listen to you."[16]

The hurtful insult and the conversation stopper stigmatize people instead of critiquing ideas. As Goffman suggests, stigmatization takes "an individual who might have been received easily in ordinary social intercourse" and assigns "a trait that can obtrude itself upon attention and turn those of us whom he meets away from him, breaking the claim that his other attributes have on us." As a result, he is "reduced in our minds from a whole and usual person to a tainted, discounted one." Legal scholar Lee Bollinger echoes these observations: "To have it said that you were once a communist sympathizer, a fascist, an atheist, or a liar can make you, at least in most quarters within the society, socially and economically a pariah, as destitute as if you had been thrown in prison and fined." Bollinger also suggests "a good case could be made for the proposition that the power of social intolerance exceeds that of legal intolerance."[17]

Confident pluralism rejects stigmatizing others through our speech. At the same time, it requires us to distinguish between stigmatizing and causing offense. Recall from the previous chapter that the civic aspiration of tolerance includes the space to make moral judgments. The liberal progressive must be able to say that the conservative moralist holds a view that he finds wrong, misguided, or immoral. And vice versa. Those assertions will likely cause offense. But they are an important part of the effort to coexist with deep and genuine differences and to allow for people to be persuaded and to change their minds.

Moral judgments can focus on ideas and beliefs rather than on people. They can avoid stigmatizing others, but they will not avoid causing offense. We fall short of the aspirations of tolerance, humility, and patience when we stigmatize others. But we risk a false tolerance—and a false humility—if we insist that nobody can be offended.

TOWARD LIVING SPEECH

We should not underestimate the power and significance of our words, or what is at stake in our language. Law professor James Boyd White suggests that "practically everything" is at stake, "including both the integrity of the individual person and the quality of our larger culture and polity." White elaborates on this idea in a powerful passage in his book, *Living Speech*:

> Each of us is partly made by the world we inhabit; this means that our most private and personal and apparently independent choices, the roots of our imagination, may be corrupted by something wrong, or evil, or demeaning, or trivializing in our world, which we have internalized. This in turn means that our choices in the world of speech, and those of others, ought not be granted perfect and unquestioned authority, either on the grounds that speech is harmless or that more speech is always all to the good.

As White concludes: "What we say, and what others say, matters enormously to all of us. It is a form of action."[18]

I wonder how many of us have ever thought about White's challenge, let alone taken it seriously. If we did, our tweets and Facebook posts might look different. Some of us might better reflect tolerance, humility, and patience in our conversations across difference. Others of us might at least start having those conversations.

Confident pluralism's speech imperative is:

> We should take steps to soften our tone and move out of our echo chambers. We should choose to avoid the hurtful insult and the conversation stopper. Living speech, even in the midst of real and painful differences, can be one of our most important bridges to one another.

Finally, as a coda to this chapter on what we *say*, the speech imperative might also affect how we *listen*. The aspirations of confident pluralism suggest a shared responsibility between speakers and hearers. We will inevitably encounter the bully and his hurtful insults and conversation stoppers. We will also encounter other forms of harmful speech—words that trivialize or brutalize the people and beliefs that we cherish. What then? We can still choose to respond with tolerance, humility, and patience.

We can also choose to listen without jumping immediately to defensiveness. Sometimes we prematurely halt dialogue with overly defensive claims of persecution or victimhood. Take the ongoing conflict between religious liberty and gay rights. Even though we frequently see the bully hurling the conversation stopper toward religious believers (with words like *close-minded*, *intolerant*, and *bigot*), many religious believers are far too quick to respond to these words or certain political or social pressures with charges of "persecution." Law professor Susan Stabile rightly observes that "failure to respect one's religion is not persecution." In a deeply divided society, not all disrespectful words and not all political decisions that disadvantage religious believers will rise to the level of persecution.

Jumping too quickly to unwarranted defensive language can also wall off relationships and end dialogue.[19]

Speaking well and listening well are not intuitive for everyone. They will often take practice and patience. They will require slowing down our social media impulses, making more drafts of the written word, and taking more pauses before the spoken word. None of this will be easy. But the coming years will give us plenty of opportunities to try.

CHAPTER 7

collective action

PROTESTS, BOYCOTTS, AND STRIKES

The "Boycott Hobby Lobby" plea lit up social media in the summer of 2014, after the Supreme Court concluded that the Religious Freedom Restoration Act entitled the national arts and crafts chain to an exemption from the requirement to cover birth control under the Affordable Care Act. The Twittersphere was outraged. Celebrity endorsements of a Hobby Lobby boycott proliferated. Even *Star Trek*'s George Takei weighed in, calling the Hobby Lobby decision a "stunning setback for women's reproductive rights" and suggesting that "the only way such companies ever learn to treat people with decency and tolerance is to hit them where it counts—in their pocketbooks."[1]

The boycott rhetoric is not limited to Hobby Lobby. Boycott Chick-fil-A (for their traditional views on marriage)! Boycott Disney (for their progressive views on marriage)! Boycott Abercrombie & Fitch (for their provocative clothing and advertisements)! One problem with these culture wars boycotts is that they seldom work. They are relatively ineffective because consumer preferences are more determined by other factors. Hobby Lobby probably doesn't lose much business from scrapbooking liberals. Abercrombie & Fitch doesn't worry about an exodus of religious conservatives who would otherwise outfit their wardrobes with the company's spring line. As commentator Megan McArdle has noted, "Almost all boycotts fail, but especially those staged as proxy battles in the culture wars." Referring specifically to the Hobby

Lobby boycott, McArdle observed, "The overlap between the people in my Facebook feed proclaiming a boycott and the people in my Facebook feed whom I know to be frequenters of crafting stores is basically zero."[2]

Sometimes the boycott rhetoric has more serious implications. Consider recent efforts to enact state religious freedom laws that might have extended protections to religious business owners who do not want to provide services at same-sex weddings. When Arizona was considering such a bill, the state confronted boycott threats from powerful corporations ranging from Delta Airlines to the NFL. A year later, Indiana faced similar threats from Angie's List, Salesforce, and—not to be outdone by the social justice aspirations of its sports counterpart—the NCAA.[3]

All of these actual and threatened boycotts are undoubtedly legal. But acknowledging their legality leaves unanswered questions about our civic aspirations: how should we think about tolerance, humility, and patience in the context of collective action? In some ways, the challenge to embody these civic aspirations is even more difficult when we move from individual speech to forms of collective action. That is the subject of this chapter.

Let's begin by recalling the distinction between confident pluralism's *constitutional commitments* and its *civic practices*. The public forum requirement from chapter 3 emphasized that we must have the *right* to engage in some forms of collective action in a world of confident pluralism—for example, we must be free to protest on public streets and sidewalks. But there is a separate question of whether and how we *should* engage in this kind of activity.

The civic practices in this chapter focus on three kinds of collective action: protests, boycotts, and strikes. Protests call attention to a problem or a policy. Boycotts discourage consumers or citizens from patronizing businesses or using certain products or services. Strikes mobilize employees seeking changes from their employers.[4]

Sometimes collective action is directed at government actors— protests outside of government offices, boycotts of cities, or strikes against government employers. The right to direct collective action against the government is one of the fundamental aspects of our

American democracy. But what happens when collective action is directed against other private citizens or the groups and institutions that they form? We can think of wide-ranging examples: fast food workers striking against their restaurant employers, Occupiers targeting Wall Street businesses, anti-abortionists protesting abortion clinics, and consumers boycotting companies.

Collective action directed at private actors raises an inherent and perhaps irresolvable tension within confident pluralism. On the one hand, it can draw attention to voices or perspectives that would otherwise go unnoticed. For example, in most business contexts, an individual consumer who disagrees with a corporate policy will have little chance of capturing the attention of the business, let alone effecting the desired change. That is also true in many cases of the relationship between individual workers and their employers (especially larger employers). Collective action by consumers or workers amplifies voices. That amplification can increase public visibility, but it can also exert economic force on a business. At the limits, the economic force can be so great that the employer must either change or shutter its doors.[5]

These possibilities are perhaps most explicit in the labor context, where boycotts, strikes, and other forms of collective action are built into our labor laws. The 1914 Clayton Act protects workers who form organizations "instituted for the purpose of mutual help." The National Labor Relations Act of 1935 (also known as the Wagner Act) introduced statutory protections for union organizing and other forms of concerted activity—including the right to strike. This kind of collective action against private employers is designed to give workers increased leverage at the bargaining table. The right to strike also brings a more direct and immediate harm to the employer than a consumer boycott: it denies the employer the means of production or service.[6]

The potential harms of strikes and boycotts reveal the tension that some forms of collective action pose for confident pluralism. Collective action that seeks to bend another's will is difficult to reconcile with tolerance, humility, and patience. When directed against other private citizens and institutions, some forms of collective action may be inconsistent, or at least less consistent, with the aspirations of confident pluralism.

How might we begin to analyze different forms of collective action within confident pluralism? One possible distinction is a sensitivity to power imbalances. When a minority viewpoint lacks the political or social clout to be heard, some form of collective action might be the only practical recourse. A similar logic underlies the protections for collective action in the labor context: without the right to strike or bargain collectively, workers would often go unheard by management.

Another consideration builds from a worry about monopoly power. Nothing about a monopoly inherently violates the aspirations of confident pluralism. In any given situation, it is conceptually possible that everyone subject to a monopoly has voluntarily reached the same views, and that meaningful exit opportunities are preserved for those who change their minds. But the fact of pluralism in our society—the actual existence of our deeply held differences—cautions us against taking such a monopoly at face value. It could be that dissenting voices have been silenced rather than persuaded. It could be that exit opportunities are more illusory than real.[7]

The preceding observations suggest we might view collective action differently in different settings. In circumstances where diverse private institutions reflect our pluralistic society, we might conclude that collective action should be permissible or perhaps even normatively encouraged. However, our approach might shift when these institutions assume certain quasi-monopolistic characteristics. In those circumstances, confident pluralism could lend greater support to collective action by consumers and citizens representing minority viewpoints against majoritarian norms. Conversely, it might discourage collective action that harnesses majoritarian power to squelch dissenting viewpoints. The precise line-drawing will be fuzzy. But we can work toward some guiding principles. Consider the following case study from the civil rights era.

THE CLAIBORNE COUNTY BOYCOTT

In 1966 African Americans comprised more than three-fourths of the population of Port Gibson, a small town in Claiborne County, Mississippi. But local officials denied blacks the right to vote, prohibited them from using public accommodations, and restricted employment in both the public and private sectors.[8]

That March, a group of black Port Gibson citizens presented to white officials a list of twenty-one demands for equal rights and racial justice. They expressed hope that they would not have to "resort to the kind of peaceful demonstrations and selective buying campaigns which have had to be used in other communities." That kind of effort "takes manpower, time and energy which could be better directed at solving these problems which exist in Port Gibson and Claiborne County by mutual cooperation and efforts at tolerant understanding." But the letter continued: "this sort of thing is inevitable unless there can be real progress toward giving all citizens their equal rights. There seems to be no other alternative."[9]

White officials ignored the petition. As one white business-owner later explained, "They were demanding too much too quickly." That April, several hundred black citizens gathered at the First Baptist Church and voted unanimously to boycott white merchants in Claiborne County. To encourage as many citizens as possible to participate, the boycotters employed "store watchers" to stand outside white-owned stores and record the names of any blacks who violated the boycott. Those names were later read at the county NAACP meetings and the individuals branded as traitors.[10]

The first three years of the boycott were mostly peaceful. Things took a turn for the worse on April 18, 1969, when a white police officer shot and killed a young black man named Roosevelt Jackson. Large crowds gathered around the hospital where Jackson had died and at the church that held his body. As community tensions escalated, Port Gibson police called for reinforcement from the State Highway Patrol. The mayor ordered a dusk-to-dawn curfew.[11]

The next day, Charles Evers, field secretary of the NAACP and brother to slain civil rights activist Medgar Evers, addressed a group of black citizens assembled at the First Baptist Church. Evers then led a march to the courthouse, where he demanded the discharge of the entire Port Gibson police force. When authorities refused that demand, Evers doubled down on the boycott and promised that blacks who ignored it would be "disciplined" by their own people. Two days later, he addressed another crowd of several hundred people and again called for the removal of the police force and for a total boycott of all white-owned businesses in Claiborne County. At one point, Evers purportedly warned the African American audience: "If we catch any of you going in any of them racist stores, we're gonna break your damn neck."[12]

In October 1969 white merchants sued the boycotters, seeking damages for their lost earnings and an injunction against further boycotts. In 1976 the trial court found that the boycott had illegally used "tactics designed to keep the black people of Claiborne County out of the white-owned businesses through the use of threats, intimidation, abusive language, ridicule, coercion and, in some cases, outright violence." The court awarded the merchants $1.25 million in lost earnings and placed an injunction on the boycott. The boycotters appealed. In 1980 the Mississippi Supreme Court rejected their appeal, finding no instance in which "free speech guaranteed by the First Amendment includes in its protection the right to commit crime."[13]

Two years later—almost twenty years after the boycotts had begun—the US Supreme Court unanimously reversed the Mississippi Supreme Court. The Court recognized that some boycotters had occasionally engaged in actual or threatened violence. But it distinguished the vast majority of the boycott as nonviolent activity fully protected under the First Amendment.[14]

The Claiborne County boycott illustrates some of the tensions that collective action raises for confident pluralism. Boycotts rely on economic and social pressure to accomplish their objectives. Rather than seeking to persuade, their warning to businesses and business owners is that the absence of change will lead to the loss of revenue and potential harm to reputation. But we can still draw distinctions between social and economic coercion on the one hand, and direct or threatened violence, on the other. The Claiborne County boycott was mostly peaceful, and the Supreme Court rightly isolated acts of violence from the majority of the boycott activities. Similarly, protests that involve peaceful protesters who are not physically blocking access to a business differ from those where protesters block access, destroy property, or threaten physical violence.

The Claiborne County boycott also asks us to think with more precision about what we mean by "majoritarian power." I suggested earlier in this chapter that we might evaluate the role of collective action within confident pluralism by examining when consumers and citizens represent minority viewpoints against majoritarian norms. How does this inquiry play out in the Claiborne County boycott, where African Americans were a numerical majority and yet politically marginalized? What does this mean in terms of power, coercion, and the role of collective action within the vision of confident pluralism?

The high percentage of African Americans in the local population enabled the boycott to exert economic coercion. White merchants would not have cared if only a small and insignificant segment of their customer base had participated. Accordingly, the demographic influence of African Americans represented a form of power. But that power cannot be situated apart from the broader political context in which it arose. As law professor Gary Minda has observed, in the Claiborne County boycott, "the boycotting group is an insular minority" that has "been denied access to the American political process." In those circumstances, Professor Minda suggests that "boycott may be the only way for the group to preserve the group's norms from being thwarted by contrary societal norms." A boycott can also give rise to a voice for social change that would otherwise have gone unheard.[15]

The Claiborne County boycott also raises the issue of coerced participation in protests. Charles Evers's threats of physical violence against black citizens who patronized the Claiborne Hard-

ware Store clearly fall beyond the boundaries of confident pluralism. But we might also worry that the store watchers used social
pressure—a kind of stigmatizing—to ensure that black citizens of
Claiborne County joined their boycott. Collective action most consistent with confident pluralism enlists participation voluntarily
rather than through social pressure. That is particularly true for
collective action in smaller and more insular communities, where
one's decision whether to participate is likelier to be scrutinized.
The stigmatizing pressure to join a boycott of the local coffee shop
in a small town may be far more acute than the pressure to join a
national boycott of Starbucks.

THE MOZILLA BOYCOTT

Stigma plays an important role not only among the participants of
collective action, but also with its targets. Just ask Brendan Eich,
the creator of the JavaScript programming language and cofounder
of Mozilla, the company that created the popular Internet browser
Firefox. In March of 2014, Eich was named the CEO of the Mozilla
Corporation. Following news of his appointment, some gay rights
supporters drew attention to a $1,000 political contribution that
Eich had made to the 2008 campaign for California Proposition 8,
a ballot initiative establishing that "only marriage between a man
and a woman is valid or recognized in California." After learning of
Eich's contribution, the online dating service OKCupid called for
a boycott of Mozilla's Firefox browser, which led to other calls for
boycotts. Within days, Eich stepped down from his position and re-
signed from the Mozilla Corporation.[16]

The philosopher John Stuart Mill spoke of similar circumstances
long before the days of Internet boycotts.

It is the opinions men entertain, and the feelings they cherish,
respecting those who disown the beliefs they deem important,
which makes this country not a place of mental freedom. For
a long time past, the chief mischief of the legal penalties is that
they strengthen the social stigma. It is that stigma which is really

effective. . . . [For most people], opinion, on this subject, is as efficacious as law; men might as well be imprisoned, as excluded from the means of earning their bread.

Mill's argument loses some force in contemporary American society. Most people who are "excluded from the means of earning their bread" as a result of social stigma will be able to secure *some* other form of employment (although Eich remained unemployed over a year after leaving Mozilla).[17]

But we should not miss Mill's point about social stigma. That stigma seems to be what drove the OKCupid boycott. The boycotters were not trying to change a practice or policy at Mozilla. By all accounts, the company is pretty gay-friendly, and Eich himself had never garnered criticism for his treatment of gay and lesbian employees. The goal of the OKCupid boycott was to get rid of Brendan Eich for his beliefs. It eschewed dialogue in favor of stigmatizing, and its ultimate target was an individual.[18]

Mozilla's response to the boycott might also fairly be subject to critique. In the midst of forcing out Eich, the company asserted that it "believes both in equality and freedom of speech" and that its "organizational culture reflects diversity and inclusiveness." Mozilla purported to "welcome contributions from everyone regardless of age, culture, ethnicity, gender, gender-identity, language, race, sexual orientation, geographical location and religious views." The *Atlantic*'s Conor Friedersdorf puzzled over this "vexing" messaging: "agree or disagree, they aren't being welcoming of 'everyone.'" Popular blogger Andrew Sullivan was more direct, labeling Mozilla's actions "McCarthyism applied by civil actors" and "the definition of intolerance."[19]

On the other hand, *New York Times* columnist Ross Douthat rightly notes that the ultimate decision to force out Eich was Mozilla's to make:

Pluralism is not a one-way street: If you want (as I do) a culture where Catholic schools and hospitals and charities are free to be Catholic, where evangelical-owned businesses don't have to pay for sterilizations and the days-after pill, where churches and synagogues and mosques don't have to worry about their tax-exempt status if they criticize "sexual modernity," you also have to acknowledge the rights of non-religious institutions of all sorts to define their own missions in ways that might make an outspoken social conservative the wrong choice for an important position within their hierarchies.[20]

Douthat's observation resonates with the give-and-take of confident pluralism and acknowledges the importance of institutional pluralism. It is also likely that most consumer boycotts today—and particularly most culture wars boycotts—occur in reasonably pluralistic settings. OKCupid's boycott against Mozilla led to Eich's removal, which then prompted some conservatives to call for a boycott of Mozilla. A year later, Eich is not the only one hurting—the market share of Mozilla's Firefox browser is down sharply and at its lowest since 2006.[21]

In addition to counter-boycotts, boycotts can also be offset by sympathetic fundraising campaigns. When a bakery that refused on religious grounds to provide services to a same-sex wedding faced boycotts and civil fines, religious conservatives responded with a fundraising campaign that raised tens of thousands of dollars for the bakery owners. (After the fundraising website GoFundMe booted that fundraising campaign, some religious conservatives called for a boycott of GoFundMe.) Social media amplifies all of these boycotts, counter-boycotts, and fundraising campaigns. Facebook has hundreds of boycott pages from across the ideological spectrum. Naturally, there are also movements to boycott Facebook.[22]

The Mozilla story raises another question: the extent to which we should take seriously the expressive and moral claims of for-profit corporations. Progressives and conservatives both argue this point inconsistently. Many progressives were quick to defend Mozilla's moral expression (and that of large corporations like Apple in the debate over Indiana's religious freedom law) but view Hobby Lobby's claims less favorably. Conversely, conservatives who ardently defended Hobby Lobby were quick to critique Mozilla and Apple. Whatever conclusion we reach as a society about the expressive and moral claims of for-profit corporations, it ought to apply across the ideological spectrum.[23]

Confident pluralism does not offer a clear prescription for how we should think about the Mozilla boycott or those boycotts that are sure to follow. It may be that these kinds of boycotts and the responses that they trigger are perfectly reasonable forms of engagement. As Douthat observes, "A healthy pluralism inevitably involves community norms and community policing in some form." On the other hand, we might worry about the manner in which social stigma operates through these forms of collective action.[24]

Others have expressed concern about the stigma associated with the Mozilla boycott. In April 2014, a group of fifty-eight well-known supporters of same-sex marriage issued a statement titled "Freedom to Marry, Freedom to Dissent: Why We Must Have Both." The statement denounced the "deeply illiberal impulse" to mute objectors to same-sex marriage, and called such efforts "both wrong in principle and poor as politics." Referring specifically to the targeting of Eich for his beliefs, the statement drew a historical parallel:

> We strongly believe that opposition to same-sex marriage is wrong, but the consequence of holding a wrong opinion should not be the loss of a job. Inflicting such consequences on others is sadly ironic in light of our movement's hard-won victory over a social order in which LGBT people were fired, harassed, and socially marginalized for holding unorthodox opinions.

The statement warned of "a worrisome turn toward intolerance and puritanism among some supporters of gay equality" that represented an "abandonment of the core liberal values of debate and diversity." And acknowledging the fact of pluralism, the statement concluded: "LGBT Americans can and do demand to be treated fairly. But we also recognize that absolute agreement on any issue does not exist."[25]

COLLECTIVE ACTION ASPIRATIONS

Confident pluralism not only suggests when and where we might engage in collective action; it also speaks to the *manner* of our engagement. Do we use profanity and name-calling on the picket line? Do we scream condemnation at women entering abortion clinics? Do we castigate Chick-fil-A as bigoted and homophobic? Our constitutional commitments should allow for each of these expressive actions. But our civic aspirations suggest that our collective action, like our speech, will sometimes assume a different posture.

Confident pluralism's collective action imperative is that:

> Boycotts, strikes, and protests against private actors are in most cases compatible with confident pluralism. When we engage in these forms of collective action, we should bear in mind the civic aspirations of tolerance, humility, and patience.

Collective action helps individual voices join together to receive a hearing they might not otherwise receive. But it can also fall short of the aspirations of confident pluralism. These inherent tensions leave the collective action imperative somewhat underspecified. Even though its actual applications will need to be worked out in specific contexts, the aspirations of tolerance, humility, and patience can direct our collective action toward a more confident pluralism.

CHAPTER 8

common GROUND
RELATIONSHIPS ACROSS DIFFERENCE

This book has focused on how we can live together in a pluralistic society in spite of our deep and profound differences. In some ways, its goal has been the modest one of coexistence. But confident pluralism's civic aspirations of tolerance, humility, and patience can also facilitate creative partnerships across difference. That brings us to the common ground imperative.

STILL LEARNING FROM JERRY AND LARRY

We met Jerry and Larry in chapter 5. They in many ways fell short of the aspirations of confident pluralism. But they may nevertheless have something to teach us.

Jerry Falwell died on May 15, 2007. Five days later, Larry Flynt published an essay in the *Los Angeles Times*. He recounted a surprising turn of events, sometime after the Campari spoof, when he and Jerry appeared together on the *Larry King Show*. At some point during the show, Jerry leaned over to give Larry an awkward but apparently heartfelt embrace. Shortly thereafter, Jerry unexpectedly paid a visit to Larry's office: "We talked for two hours, with the latest issues of *Hustler* neatly stacked on my desk in front of him. He suggested that we go around the country debating, and I agreed." Here is how Larry concluded his tribute to Jerry:

> In the years that followed and up until his death, he'd come to see me every time he was in Califor-

fornia. We'd have interesting philosophical conversations. We'd exchange personal Christmas cards. He'd show me pictures of his grandchildren. I was with him in Florida once when he complained about his health and his weight, so I suggested that he go on a diet that had worked for me. I faxed a copy to his wife when I got back home.

The truth is, the reverend and I had a lot in common. He was from Virginia, and I was from Kentucky. His father had been a bootlegger, and I had been one too in my 20s before I went into the Navy. We steered our conversations away from politics, but religion was within bounds. He wanted to save me and was determined to get me out of "the business." . . .

He was definitely selling brimstone religion and would do anything to add another member to his mailing list. But in the end, I knew what he was selling, and he knew what I was selling, and we found a way to communicate. . . .

I'll never admire him for his views or his opinions. To this day, I'm not sure if his television embrace was meant to mend fences, to show himself to the public as a generous and forgiving preacher or merely to make me uneasy, but the ultimate result was one I never expected and was just as shocking a turn to me as was winning that famous Supreme Court case: We became friends.

It is fair to say that Jerry and Larry are unlikely models for confident pluralism. But if they can move toward its aspirations of tolerance, humility, and patience, then maybe we can, too.[1]

NO HAPPY ENDINGS?

Or maybe not. As Larry said, the truth is that he and Jerry had a lot in common—geography, gender, age, class, and experience. That is a lot more than many of us have in common with each other. And that means that confident pluralism might ask a lot more of us than it did of Jerry and Larry. How, for example, do we practically shape the civic aspirations of tolerance, patience, and humility? How, in the midst of so much difference, do we secure agreement about the need for confident pluralism itself? How do we encourage the hard work of relationships across difference? What if not enough people care?

These questions take on an even bleaker tone when we examine the difficulties of pursuing dialogue across difference. Consider, for example, political scientist Robert Putnam's critique of "the optimistic hypothesis that if we have more contact with people of other ethnic and racial backgrounds (or at least more contact in the right circumstances), we will all begin to trust one another more." Putnam observes that most empirical studies suggest just the opposite: "for various reasons—but above all, contention over limited resources—diversity fosters out-group distrust and in-group solidarity." In fact, Putnam's research suggests that the problem is even worse than these studies suggest: diversity not only fosters out-group distrust, but "in-group trust, too, is lower in more diverse settings." He concludes that "inhabitants of diverse communities tend to withdraw from collective life, to distrust their neighbours, regardless of the colour of their skin, to withdraw even from close friends, to expect the worst from their community and its leaders, to volunteer less, give less to charity and work on community projects less often, to register to vote less, to agitate for social reform *more*, but have less faith that they can actually make a difference, and to huddle unhappily in front of the television."[2]

All of this sounds rather dreary, but Putnam ends with a note of cautious optimism. Even though "in the short run there is a trade-off between diversity and community," there may be ways to pursue strategies that over time "can ameliorate that tradeoff." Turning to the policy questions surrounding immigration reform, Putnam concludes:

> It would be unfortunate if a politically correct progressivism were to deny the reality of the challenge to social solidarity posed by diversity. It would be equally unfortunate if an ahistorical and ethnocentric conservatism were to deny that addressing that challenge is both feasible and desirable. . . . The task of becoming comfortable with diversity will not be easy or quick, but it will be

speeded by our collective efforts and in the end well worth the effort.

Or, perhaps more bluntly: we're stuck with all of this difference, and we need to find a way to live with it. Confident pluralism is one possibility. It may not work, and it may fail to persuade. But it may also be the best we've got.[3]

FINDING COMMON GROUND

Jack Danforth, the former Missouri senator, shares a poignant example of confident pluralism in his recent book on religion and politics. Senator Danforth introduces us to Loretto Wagner, a Catholic woman who served as president of Missouri Citizens for Life and "dedicated herself to overturning the effects of *Roe v. Wade*," and B. J. Isaacson-Jones, who at the time was the director of Missouri's largest abortion clinic. Isaacson-Jones "requested a meeting of pro-choice and pro-life leaders to discuss shared interests such as preventing unwanted pregnancies." That meeting led to monthly dinners and an informal group that participants called "Common Ground." Senator Danforth continues:

> As Loretto Wagner describes the dinners, "We talked for hours. We talked about our families and really became friends. I never thought I would be able to say that. We realized that these are human beings with feelings. A magical thing happened between all of us." The new friendships created what Loretto calls "an atmosphere of trust" in which participants could discuss their differences in a civil manner. Positive results followed. Isaacson-Jones called Loretto about a ten-year-old who initially came to the clinic for an abortion only to decide to keep the baby. Since the girl had a complicated pregnancy, Isaacson-Jones asked Loretto to find a caregiver to look after the girl while her mother was at work. Loretto raised money to pay for the caregiver. The baby was subsequently put up for adoption. The Common Ground partners worked together to support state legislation to pay for pregnant drug addicts. The abortion clinic opened on premises adoption services to provide an alternative to un-

wanted pregnancies. In the grand scheme of the long raging debate over abortion, none of these achievements were earth shak-
ing, but each showed that people who seek common ground can
find it, and in finding it they can change the culture of a community.

I suspect that many people on both sides of the abortion debate
will find this example challenging, and some will find it unworkable. But it demonstrates the possibility of partnership across deep
and painful differences for the sake of shared interests. That doesn't
give us a common good, but it pushes us toward common ground
where we can find it.[4]

As difficult as it may be to find common ground on an individual
level, bridging *institutional* difference can pose even greater challenges. Institutional partnership is particularly difficult at the national level. It is perhaps more attainable at the local level.

One example comes from Portland, Oregon. In the spring of
2008, Christian evangelist Kevin Palau approached Sam Adams,
Portland's openly gay mayor. Palau recognized that evangelical
Christians in the city were known more for what they were against
than for what they were for. Seeking to build relationships with
his community, he decided to do the "obvious thing" and went to
Mayor Adams to ask what religious believers could do to help the
city.[5]

Adams was not particularly fond of evangelicals, but he needed
volunteers to help address Portland's educational, environmental,
and health needs. He knew that evangelicals viewed his sexual conduct as sinful ("I'm sure that's Kevin's view"), but he "decided to
set that difference aside and go ahead with the partnership for the
sake of mobilizing people to aid his city." For Adams, "a fundamental challenge is to overcome the way we've all been conditioned . . .
that if we disagree, then we must hate each other." The very real
question for Adams and Palau was: "Can you simultaneously disagree on some things and act together on others?"[6]

Three years after Palau and Adams first met, 26,000 volunteers from 500 local churches were "helping the city do everything from renovating parks, to counseling victims of sex trafficking and feeding the homeless." One church focuses its efforts on Roosevelt High School, whose students are primarily low-income students of color. As a 2013 *New York Times* article observed: "Throughout the school year, members of SouthLake Church in the prosperous suburb of West Linn serve as tutors at Roosevelt. A former NFL quarterback in the congregation, Neil Lomax, helps coach the football team. SouthLake pays for another member, Heather Huggitt, 26, to work full time at Roosevelt helping to meet the material needs of students who often lack sufficient food, clothing and school supplies."[7]

Both Palau and Adams emphasize the importance of relationship across difference in addressing these problems. Adams stresses the significance not only of relationships between church leaders and city officials, but also of those between individual parishioners and city employees. He has not forgotten his significant differences with Palau. But Adams did not want those differences to get in the way of their similar goals. Palau agrees, and said so in a 2014 dialogue with Adams: "Precisely because we may not find common ground on everything, let's work all the harder to find common ground on what we can. We all care about a more livable Portland." The possibilities in Portland depended upon finding common ground, even in the absence of a shared common good.[8]

BRIDGING RELATIONAL DISTANCE

The stories recounted in this chapter depend in part on relationships that overcame distance. We might be inclined to focus on the bridging of *ideological* distance—to think that the actors in these stories in some ways grew closer to one another's views or worked toward compromise. But that interpretation would misread these stories. In fact, we see little indication of either compromise or increased affinity for another's viewpoint. Loretto and B. J. did not change their views about abortion. Jerry didn't start subscribing to Hustler, and Larry didn't begin donating to Jerry's Moral Majority. And Kevin and Sam did not reach agreement about their beliefs about sexuality. Meaningful relationships within confident plural-ism do not depend on compromise or change bridging ideological distance.

But all of these actors overcame distance in another way: through shared experiences and common enterprises. In other words, they bridged *relational* distance. Loretto and B. J. worked with each other on a tangible policy initiative. Jerry and Larry em-barked on a speaking tour together. Kevin and Sam partnered to improve Portland. Each of the actors in these stories benefited from the civility, trust, and friendship that emerged through their shared experiences. Confident pluralism holds out this possibility for the rest of us.

Our efforts to bridge relational distance will not be without chal-lenges. One of these challenges is our *speech*. Neither the hurtful insult nor the conversation stopper bridges relational distance; if anything, they are likely to increase it. That is one reason that Pro-fessor White's observations about speech are so important: our words can either help or hinder our relationships. The early years of Jerry and Larry's relationship were laced with hurtful insults and conversation stoppers. It is unlikely that they would have found common ground without moving past those forms of destructive speech. B. J. and Loretto were not speaking destructively to one another—their problem was that they weren't speaking at all. And their partnership toward common ground depended upon dia-logue.

A second challenge to overcoming relational distance is our *un-familiarity* with one another. B. J. and Loretto learned each other's names, faces, and stories. Their relationship required them to move beyond the faceless "other side." In fact, our real-life interactions are too often encumbered not only by unfamiliarity, but also by anonymity. One reason that the Dave Principle works so well in our online interactions is that we often don't even know the names of the people that we're critiquing, excoriating, or dismissing. And even when we do know names, we often don't know people. It is a lot harder to fire snarky tweets at people you will actually see in real life. That to me is one of the benefits of academic conferences. Many of the Twitter handles I encounter online belong to people with whom I will share a drink or a meal in the coming months. And that matters to our civility.[9]

Finally, our *physical separation* can be a significant impediment to our ability to bridge relational distance. An adequate reflection about physical separation would easily fill the pages of another book, but we can make a few passing observations. Notice how physical proximity mattered in the stories recounted in this chapter. Loretto and B. J. lived in the same city but had to find their way to the same room. The same is true for Kevin and Sam. Jerry and Larry lived far from one another, but their connections deepened through a series of face-to-face encounters. Sharing literal common ground facilitated relational common ground.

These opportunities are not always available in a world where online communication increasingly substitutes for actual meetings or in-person friendships, and offline communication is complicated by divided neighborhoods, long commutes, and poor city planning. Take the idyllic notion of the "town square." What is now usually just a metaphor was once an actual space in most towns. But as urban planner Charles Marohn has noted, "In suburbia, there is no town square." Instead, as reporter Jim Dalrymple has observed: "Single-family homes proliferate in residential areas; strip malls and parking lots dominate commercial sections. Those two types of development rarely mix, and everything is designed to be accessed by car." As a consequence, there is no place for people to meet.[10]

When we are honest with ourselves, our efforts to pursue relationships are complicated by indifference as much as they are by poor city planning. We often limit our interactions in those spaces to people we know. It takes effort to bridge unnatural connections or to drive across town to meet someone outside of our comfort zone. Sometimes it takes effort to walk next door to greet our neighbor.[11]

Focusing on our speech, overcoming anonymity, and lessening our physical separation are practical ways to move toward common ground. The common ground imperative is that:

Even in the midst of our deepest differences, we might share enough common ground to maintain the possibility of relationship across those differences. We can bridge relational distance even when we cannot bridge ideological distance.

The common ground imperative is not an unworkable pipe dream. It plays out in the lives of Jerry and Larry, B. J. and Loretto, and Sam and Kevin. It unfolds in the unlikely friendship between Chick-fil-A founder Dan Cathy and Campus Pride founder Shane Windmeyer ("After months of personal phone calls, text messages and in-person meetings, I am coming out in a new way, as a friend of Chick-fil-A's president and COO, Dan Cathy"). It manifests in the surprising relationship between former Republican senator Tom Coburn and President Barack Obama ("It may be Washington's most unlikely friendship, but it's a lesson that political opposites can work together in highly partisan and dysfunctional times"). It exists through relationships that you and I have with neighbors, colleagues, and collaborators. But the common ground imperative is not a given—it will not happen without deliberate effort and hard work across difference.[12]

CONCLUSION

Confident pluralism argues that we can, and we must, learn to live with each other in spite of our deep differences. It requires a tolerance for dissent, a skepticism of government orthodoxy, and a willingness to endure strange and even offensive ways of life. Confident pluralism asks that those charged with enforcing our laws do better in preserving and strengthening our constitutional commitments to voluntary groups, public forums, and certain kinds of generally available funding. It also challenges each of us to live out the aspirations of tolerance, humility, and patience in our civic practices.

Confident pluralism does not give us the American Dream. But it might help us avoid the American Nightmare. How might we go about pursuing that possibility? These final pages sketch a vision.

THE CONSTITUTIONAL COMMITMENTS OF CONFIDENT PLURALISM

Confident pluralism will not succeed without constitutional commitments that sufficiently protect us from an overreaching state that seeks to control and suppress difference and dissent. One of the primary arguments of this book is that our current constitutional framework falls short and is headed in a wrong direction. In other words, we *must* alter the course of our legal framework for confident pluralism to be a sustainable political possibility. In the first part of this book, I sketched the problems with the current doctrine and gestured toward ways to remedy those those problems. In particular, I argued that we must redefine and reimagine three aspects of constitutional doctrine: the voluntary groups requirement, the public forum requirement, and the public funding requirement. This redefinition and reimagining does not need to be invented out of whole cloth. Rather, it builds upon our modest unity, including our longstanding commitment to individual rights.

The voluntary groups requirement argues that we need stronger protections for civil society groups to create and maintain their own ways of life. The right of expressive association, which focuses primarily on the outward expression of groups, insufficiently protects these goals. It ignores the ways in which most people actually form beliefs, practices, and modes of resistance—through informal and even nonexpressive gatherings that facilitate friendships, relationships, and solidarity. As I explained in chapter 2, even those groups that qualify as expressive associations confront a vague doctrinal framework that too easily balances constitutional protections out of existence.

We need either an overhaul of the expressive association doctrine or a return to the First Amendment's right of assembly. At a minimum, the First Amendment should offer meaningful protections to the voluntary groups of civil society. Those protections are not absolute. The government properly intervenes for well-articulated compelling reasons, such as the prevention of violence. But our history includes many examples of government actors too quickly intervening without adequate justification.

The public forum requirement insists that citizens have physical and virtual spaces to come together to voice their dissent, opposition, and discontent. It is essential that government either establish and maintain those spaces or ensure that private public forums acting in its stead hold open similar possibilities. To ensure meaningful access to the public forum, it will be necessary to reformulate the current doctrinal framework, which too easily cedes control to government officials.

The public funding requirement preserves access to generally available government funding, regardless of ideology. The government has the authority to use much of its tax-generated revenue for its own purposes. But in venues that promote a diversity of viewpoints and ideas—venues like the forum for student organizations at public universities, or the federal tax exemption—government should not be permitted to demand its own orthodoxy as a condition to obtaining generally available benefits.

Each of the preceding challenges unfolds at the level of constitutional doctrine. One might reasonably ask: "What can I do about any of this?" It is a fair question—most of us are not Supreme Court justices. But even if we are not in positions of extraordinary power and influence, we are still a part of a representative democracy. We still have a choice to accept the status quo or to press more deeply into the questions that have shaped our country and that will shape it in the days ahead. Reading this book is one part of that effort. You might also take time to read the counterarguments.[1]

We can also take practical steps toward reestablishing the proper protections for confident pluralism. When federal constitutional law fails at the level of Supreme Court doctrine, there may be little that can be done outside of the Court to remedy that failure. But the beauty of our system is that it usually allows for independent protections to be advanced at the state level, whether through constitutional amendment, legislation, or policy. State and local officials are far more accessible to regular people: we can request a meeting, write a petition, or start a debate.[2]

We can also be mindful of the ways in which ordinary policy decisions often affect us to a greater extent than extraordinary constitutional decisions. For example, the denial of tax-exempt status to *Big Mama Rag* came at the hands of government employees at the Internal Revenue Service. Similar government employees do important work at the state and local level. They are ordinary citizens entrusted with a modicum of power. They are not infallible, and some of them need to be held accountable for abusing positions of trust, whether out of self-interest, prejudice, laziness, or indifference. It is up to people like you and me to ensure that government officials wield power fairly and in the best interests of our democratic society.

Finally, when we learn of officials denying meaningful protections to a voluntary group without justification, we can push back by mobilizing those around us. When we see local officials unjustly suppressing peaceful protests, or squelching dissent with a massive show of force (like the armored personnel carriers and sniper rifles that appeared in Ferguson), we can insert ourselves into the dialogue, the outrage, or even the protest itself.

THE CIVIC PRACTICES OF CONFIDENT PLURALISM

The civic practices of confident pluralism raise practical questions of how we can coexist in the midst of our deep differences. These are the questions of how we act when the law runs out—when no judge or police officer will tell us what we must do. These civic practices hinge on the aspirations of tolerance, humility, and patience. They play out in three imperatives.

The speech imperative understands that even as we preserve our differences and the right to make moral judgments, we can work to avoid the hurtful insult and the conversation stopper. We can choose to avoid stigmatizing other people. We can work toward living speech that enables relationships across our differences.

The collective action imperative recognizes that we are often better able to make our voices heard in groups rather than as individuals. Sometimes our collective action will pressure other citizens and their private institutions. Confident pluralism counsels toward tolerance, humility, and patience in these forms of collective action.

We can also choose to move beyond fleeting forms of collective action. Hashtag activism costs us little. Real activism takes commitment and inconvenience that continue long after the cameras are gone. It requires us to play the long game—to move from the sprint to the marathon. Twitter campaigns and street protests are often about the sprint. The adrenaline is flowing, the passions are high, and the filters are off. The problem with the sprint is that our fleeting outrage may not make a long-term difference, to us or to anyone else. Too often, we will vent or tweet and then forget about it. We might instead choose to channel our emotions for the hard work of the marathon.[3]

Finally, the common ground imperative reminds us that partnering both interpersonally and institutionally despite our differences can lead to common ground that benefits us all. These relationships can also reinforce our commitment to confident pluralism by reminding us of the ordinary humanity of those with whom we most disagree. Our civic practices can embody the aspirations of confident pluralism in ways that are better demonstrated than asserted. In the real world, aspirations have to move from words to actions: "I tolerate you," "I am humble," and "Look at my patience" are clunky and self-serving. But when others can *see* our tolerance, humility, and patience, we begin to create a different world.

COMMON GROUND IN CONFIDENT PLURALISM

One final story of finding common ground across difference comes from an effort to secure confident pluralism's constitutional commitments. It demonstrates common ground across difference, but it also illustrates why these constitutional commitments are important for us all.

In 2000 the Supreme Court upheld what it deemed to be "content-neutral" limitations that restricted the speech and expression of anti-abortion protesters on public sidewalks outside abortion clinics in Colorado. Justice Anthony Kennedy's dissent argued that the Court's decision left unprotected core political expression conducted "in a peaceful manner and on a profound moral issue, to a fellow citizen on a public sidewalk." You'll recall from chapter 3 that public sidewalks are paradigmatic traditional public forums.[4]

Fourteen years later, the Supreme Court decided another case involving anti-abortion protesters on public sidewalks outside abortion clinics, this time in Massachusetts. The Massachusetts restrictions in *McCullen v. Coakley* were even more severe than the Colorado restrictions. They criminalized any gathering of two or more people on public sidewalks outside abortion clinics. They prevented the plaintiff, Eleanor McCullen, from using the sidewalk outside an abortion clinic to sing or pray quietly.[5]

Like many Supreme Court cases, *McCullen* drew an avalanche of legal briefs arguing various legal theories to the justices. Many of those briefs filed in support of Ms. McCullen quoted Harvard Law School professor Laurence Tribe's assertion that the Court's earlier decision in *Hill* was "slam-dunk simple and slam-dunk wrong." Quoting Professor Tribe in a brief to the Supreme Court was not itself unusual; he is a well-known legal scholar who taught a number of the justices when they were law students. But what made his words so important in this case was that Tribe is also a staunch defender of abortion rights.[6]

Nor did the unusual alliance end there. The American Federation of Labor and Congress of Industrial Organizations (AFL-CIO) submitted a brief arguing that the sidewalk restrictions were unconstitutional. The AFL-CIO's brief cited a number of labor decisions that supported a robust public forum, and it emphasized the "vital interest in the First Amendment rights of citizens to disseminate their views on the public streets by picketing, handbilling, and engaging in other forms of protected expression."[7]

Professor Michael McConnell and I coauthored an amicus ("friend of the court") brief on behalf of a number of religious organizations. Amicus briefs are intended to provide the Court with perspectives of people and organizations who are not part of the actual litigation but who have a stake in its outcome. Our brief argued that the Massachusetts restrictions unconstitutionally infringed upon the public forum and the right of assembly. We enlisted a coalition of religious groups, some of which shared very little in common with one another. It's not every day that the United States Conference of Catholic Bishops, the Ethics and Religious Liberty Commission of the Southern Baptist Convention, and the International Society for Krishna Consciousness (the Hare Krishnas) agree with each other. But all of them (and many other groups) joined our brief, recognizing the shared importance of the public forum to their otherwise divergent interests.[8]

In June 2014 the Supreme Court struck down the Massachusetts law, in a welcome development that edges us closer to the public forum requirement. Writing in the *New York Times*, Professor Tribe praised the decision: "That I don't share Ms. McCullen's views is beside the point. The great virtue of our First Amendment is that it protects speech we hate just as vigorously as it protects speech we support."[9]

But that's not the end of the story. Days after the Supreme Court's decision, a federal district judge in North Carolina relied on *McCullen* to dismiss criminal charges against dozens of "Moral Mondays" protesters who had challenged recent actions by the North Carolina legislature. Many of those protesters were progressives, including members of Planned Parenthood who had joined the Moral Mondays protests to argue on behalf of abortion rights. They, too, benefited from the public forum requirement. That's precisely how the constitutional commitments of confident pluralism are meant to work. And in *McCullen*, a broad array of ideologically diverse people and organizations found common ground around that principle.[10]

THE CHALLENGE FOR US

The argument for confident pluralism is an argument about the future of the American experiment. Seen in this light, our confidence is not only in our own deeply held beliefs, but also in the ongoing possibility of our constitutional commitments and civic practices. In other words, confident pluralism is also a confidence in the political arrangement that we call the United States of America. It is a confidence that we retain some modicum of unity even in the midst of our vast diversity.

Many people think that our deep differences are getting deeper. But at least one reason for this perceived change is that we have allowed more voices into the conversation—we have extended the political community to encompass the people and beliefs that we actually find in our midst. Our country may have had more "coherence" of a kind in an earlier era, but a good deal of that coherence was only made possible by suppressing or excluding dissenting or unheard voices. That is not, in fact, confident pluralism. It is confidence (by some) without pluralism (for all).[11]

Our collective confidence in light of our actual differences depends on a kind of shared trust that can be bruised or even broken. But the government of "we the people" can be confident in the political solution of confident pluralism as a response to the practical problem of our deep differences. We can choose to answer the question of the possibility of coexistence differently than Rousseau. Recall the words from Justice Jackson that I quoted in chapter 1: "We apply the limitations of the Constitution with no fear that freedom to be intellectually and spiritually diverse or even contrary will disintegrate the social organization."[12]

Seventy years ago, the political commentator Walter Lippmann took on "one of the most important questions of the time" when he asked: "On what philosophical basis might America build a unified public culture, given all its diversity?" Today, we are far more diverse than when Lippmann posed his question, and we still lack an adequate answer. Or take a pair of questions that the sociologist James Davison Hunter asked over twenty years ago in a book ominously titled *Before the Shooting Begins*: "Can democratic practice today mediate differences as deep as [ours] in a manner that is in keeping with the ideals set forth in the founding documents of the American republic? Or will one side, through the tactics of power politics, simply impose its vision on all others?" Those questions, too, remain with us.[13]

The challenge of confident pluralism is how to coexist and even thrive across and in spite of our deep differences. That political solution does not collapse our differences; to the contrary, it sometimes heightens them. On careful reflection, it also suggests that our differences may well prevent us from discovering a "common good" for society. We are unlikely to reach a shared understanding about the meanings of abstract notions like equality, dignity, autonomy, morality, or justice. We are unlikely to agree upon the meaning of human flourishing or the fundamental purposes of our country and its communities.

The challenges arising out of our deep differences are not going away. But as we move toward an unknown future, we can retain some basic level of agreement about how to live with these differences. Confident pluralism offers that possibility. It will not convince everyone. It may not reshape entrenched intolerance, shallow certainty, or shortsighted impatience. But it might persuade enough of us who are confident in our own beliefs and focused on preserving our modest unity amidst our pluralism. To that end, it adds a fourth aspiration to tolerance, humility, and patience: hope.[14]

acknowledgments

This book has benefited from extended conversations and debates with a number of colleagues from various disciplines and institutions. I am grateful for advice and friendship from Susan Appleton, Barb Armacost, Will Baude, Susan Bickford, Colin Bird, Joseph Blocher, John Bowen, Kathy Bradley, Stanley Carlson-Thies, Nathan Chapman, Guy-Uriel Charles, Marion Crain, Marc DeGirolami, Kevin den Dulk, Deborah Dinner, Rebecca Dresser, Kathleen Flake, Rick Garnett, Erin Hawley, Paul Horwitz, John Infranca, Richard Kaplan, Pauline Kim, Randy Kozel, Doug Laycock, Mike Lienesch, Frank Lovett, Greg Magarian, Ian Mac-Mullen, Mac McCorkle, Trenton Merricks, Michael Moreland, Steve Monsma, Rich Mouw, Jeff Pojanowski, Jeff Powell, Neil Richards, Micah Schwartzman, Pat Shin, David Skeel, Larry Solum, Ronit Stahl, Nelson Tebbe, Mark Valeri, David VanDrunen, Kevin Walsh, and Peter Wiedenbeck. Thanks especially to Chad Flanders, Ron Levin, Chuck Mathewes, Jason Mazzone, Brian Tamanaha, Abram Van Engen, and Tim Zick for extensive comments and dialogue, and to Andy Crouch and Jeff Spinner-Halev for encouraging me to write this book.

I completed this manuscript during a fellowship at the Institute for Advanced Studies in Culture at the University of Virginia. I am thankful to James Davison Hunter for the invitation to join him for the year, and for the friendships and community that emerged during that year with James and with Leann Davis Alspaugh, Elizabeth Bickley, Carl Bowman, Joe Davis,

Emily Gum, Tony Lin, Philip Lorish, B. D. McClay, Murray Milner, Maegan Moore, James Mumford, Johann Neem, John Owen, Matt Puffer, Greg Thompson, Jay Tolson, Chad Wellmon, and Josh Yates. Thanks also to my home institution, Washington University School of Law, for supporting the opportunity for me to write this book.

My special thanks to Rick Garnett, Rosalind Alexander, and the Program on Church, State, and Society at Notre Dame School of Law for organizing a roundtable on the book, and to the participants in that event: Will Baude, Kristen Deede Johnson, Patrick Deneen, Chad Flanders, Randy Kozel, Bryan McGraw, Michael Moreland, Jeff Pojanowski, Steve Smith, Nick Wolterstorff, and Tim Zick. The critiques from this group were enormously helpful. This manuscript also benefited from workshops at Washington University School of Law, the Political Theory Colloquium at the University of North Carolina, the Institute for Advanced Studies in Culture at the University of Virginia, the Project on Religion, Pluralism, Secularism, and Law at the University of Virginia, the Center for Christianity and Scholarship at Duke University, Illinois Law School, and Suffolk Law School.

I am also thankful for informal discussions over drafts of the manuscript with friends in Cambridge, Charlottesville, Durham, New Haven, St. Louis, Washington, DC, and Winston-Salem. Special thanks to Amin Aminfar, Edward Bennett, Nathan Berkeley, Allie Brauns, Matt Bridges, Tyler Castle, Marcus Cave, Liz Chao, Chip Denton, Desiree Denton, Edward Dixon, Jon Endean, Don Flow, Griff Gatewood, Chris Hampson, Alex Harris, Alex Hartemink, Melissa Hartemink, Paul Hartge, Matthew Hawkins, Tyler Hood, Tim Keller, Rich Keshian, Warren Kinghorn, Prajwal Kulkarni, Brian Lindman, JennyLark Lindman, Shapri LoMaglio, Will McDavid, Jared Notzel, Cam Nunery, Karl Pollack, Allan Poole, Betsy Poole, Sarah Poole, Mark Ryan, Graham Scharf, Sam Speers, Stephanie Summers, Katie Thompson, Matthew Vaselkiv, Joshua Wade, Michael Wear, and Noel Weichbrodt.

I am grateful to the many professionals at the University of Chicago Press who helped bring this book to fruition. My editor, the late Chris Rhodes, skillfully blended encouragement and critique at various stages of the manuscript. The three anonymous reviewers of the manuscript offered thoughtful and generous feedback that significantly improved some of the arguments.

Some of the material in this book builds upon prior publications. The Introduction and Chapter 5 expand upon material in "A Confident Pluralism," *Southern California Law Review* 88 (2015): 587. Chapters 3 and 4 are based in part on "The First Amendment's Public Forum," *William & Mary Law Review* 56 (2015): 1159. Portions of the book develop ideas first referenced in "Virtual Assembly," *Cornell Law Review* 98 (2013): 1093; "Re-Assembling Labor," *Illinois Law Review* (2015): 1791 (with Marion Crain); "The Four Freedoms and the Future of Religious Liberty," *North Carolina Law Review* 92 (2014): 787; and "More Is More: Strengthening Free Exercise, Speech, and Association," *Minnesota Law Review* 99 (2014): 111. Some of the prose also appears in a series of articles published in *Christianity Today*. I am grateful to the editors of all of these publications for the permission to use material drawn from them.

I am indebted to the Arthur and Elizabeth Schlesinger Library on the History of Women in America at the Radcliffe Institute for Advanced Study at Harvard University, and the Albin O. Kuhn Library & Gallery at the University of Maryland, Baltimore County, for assistance with archival work on *Big Mama Rag*.

My research assistants sharpened this book in countless ways: Catherine Crane, David Dean, Jackie Fugitt, Mark Gruetzmacher, Kent Hayden, Shane Hunt, Jonathan Hwang, Mike Martinich-Sauter, Claire Melvin, Alec Moen, and Bryan Ryan. Their intelligence, humor, and work ethic give me confidence in the future of the legal profession.

I am grateful to my parents, Willie and Sandy Inazu (for the record, my mom is nowhere close to the "Sandy Principle"), and my in-laws, Skip and Melissa Young. Thanks especially to my wife, Caroline, for putting up with my distractions and idiosyncrasies while writing this book (and just generally).

This book is dedicated to my children: Lauren, Hana, and Sam. May you treat others with tolerance, humility, and patience, and may you be treated likewise.

notes

INTRODUCTION

1 Everson v. Board of Education, 330 U.S. 1 (1947).

2 Michael Feingold, "Foreman's Wake-Up Call," *Village Voice* (2004), quoted in Jonathan Haidt, *The Righteous Mind: Why Good People Are Divided by Politics and Religion* (New York: Vintage Books, 2012), 335; Jon Terbush, "On Ferguson, Stop Telling Athletes to 'Shut Up and Play,'" *The Week*, December 4, 2014, quoting Bill O'Reilly, http://theweek.com/articles/441796/ferguson-stop-telling -athletes-shut-play; Kim Geiger, "Rush Limbaugh's 'Slut' Comment Draws Rebukes from All Sides," *Los Angeles Times*, March 2, 2012; J. Bryan Lowder, "No, It's Not Too Soon to Condemn Public Figures for Being Anti-Gay," *Outward* (blog), April 7, 2014, http://www.slate.com/blogs/outward/2014/04/07/brenden_eich_s _mozilla_resignation_proves_gay_rights_are_no_longer_up_for.html; Jon Lovett, "The Culture of Shut Up," *The Atlantic*, April 7, 2014, http://www.theatlantic .com/politics/archive/2014/04/the-culture-of-shut-up/360239/.

3 N.C. Const. art. XIV, § 6; David Zucchino, "Marriage Amendment Vote Puts National Focus on North Carolina," *Los Angeles Times*, May 5, 2012. Not everyone agreed about the potential effects of the amendment. See E. Gregory Wallace, "The Sky Didn't Fall: The Meaning and Legal Effects of the North Carolina Marriage Amendment," *American University Journal of Gender Social Policy and Law* 22, no. 1 (2013): 1–45 (arguing against "predictions of dire consequences that have yet to occur—and likely never will"). In 2014 a federal district court ruled North Carolina's ban on same-sex marriage unconstitutional in General Synod of the United Church of Christ v. Resinger, 12 F.Supp.3d 790 (W.D. N.C. 2014).

4 Michael Paulson, "Colleges and Evangelicals Collide on Bias Policy," *New York Times*, June 10, 2014, A1.

5 Greg Garrison, "Amendment Banning 'Foreign Law' in Alabama Courts Passes; Will Be Added to Alabama Constitution," *Birmingham News*, November 4, 2014, http://www.al.com/news/index.ssf/2014/11/amendment_banning_foreign_law .html; Paul Horwitz, "Amendment One is Useless, Costly, and Wrong," *Huntsville Times*, October 30, 2014, http://www.al.com/opinion/index.ssf/2014/10/amend ment_one_is_useless_costl.html; Liz Farmer, "Alabama Joins Wave of States Banning Foreign Laws," Governing.com, November 4, 2014.

6 Ruth Padawer, "When Women Become Men at Wellesley," *New York Times*, October 15, 2014. In March 2015, Wellesley announced that it "will consider for admission any applicant who lives as a woman and consistently identifies as a woman." Abby McIntyre, "Wellesley's Decision to Admit Transgender Women Is Smart and Just," *Outward* (blog), March 5, 2015, http://www.slate.com/blogs/outward /2015/03/05/wellesley_college_will_consider_applications_from_transgender _women_good.html.

7 John Rawls, "The Idea of an Overlapping Consensus," *Oxford Journal of Legal Studies* 7, no. 1 (1987): 4.

8 See Robert D. Putnam, "*E Pluribus Unum*: Diversity and Community in the Twenty-first Century," *Scandinavian Political Studies* 30, no. 2 (2007): 137. For

making my basketball watching more pleasurable by their allegiances to less fortunate programs, I am indebted to David Dean, Ford Jordan, Don Fox, Ivy Pointer, Drew Hill, David Kernodle, Ruthie McGinn, Jonathan Murfee, Amit Shanker, and Ian Smith.

9 Jean-Jacques Rousseau, *The Social Contract*, trans. G. D. H. Cole (London: Dent, 1968), 114. Gabriel Arana, "Gays Hate America and Other Right-Wing Talking Points on Indiana," *Huffington Post*, April 3, 2015, quoting Mark Levin; Family Research Council, "Religious Freedom Should Not Be Held Hostage to Big Business, Family Research Council Urges Veto," press release, April 2, 2015; Tim Cook, "Pro-discrimination 'Religious Freedom' Laws Are Dangerous," *Washington Post*, March 29, 2015; Ben Kepes, "Salesforce.com Makes a Stand Against Bigotry," *Forbes*, March 26, 2015, http://www.forbes.com/sites/benkepes/2015/03/26/salesforce-com-makes-a-stand-against-bigotry/; Jon Healey, "The Backlash Against the Backlash Against Indiana's New Religious Freedom Law," *Los Angeles Times*, April 2, 2015 (describing the threats and boycotts against Memories Pizza after the owners said in response to a local television reporter's question that they would not cater a gay wedding).

10 Shadi Hamid, "The End of Pluralism," *The Atlantic*, July 23, 2014.

11 Abner S. Greene, *Against Obligation: The Multiple Sources of Authority in a Liberal Democracy* (Cambridge, MA: Harvard University Press, 2012), 23. See also Jonathan Sacks, *The Dignity of Difference: How to Avoid the Clash of Civilizations* (New York: Continuum, 2002) (arguing for the importance of taking difference seriously). For my critiques of the consensus aspirations of Rawlsian liberalism and mid-twentieth-century liberalism, see John D. Inazu, *Liberty's Refuge: The Forgotten Freedom of Assembly* (New Haven, CT: Yale University Press, 2012), 97–117 (critiquing the "liberal consensus" of mid-twentieth-century pluralist political theory), 153–62 (critiquing aspects of Rawlsian liberalism). Confident pluralism is, however, similar to Rawls in its agnosticism about the moral justifications for and moral critiques of the fact of pluralism. See John Rawls, *Political Liberalism* (New York: Columbia University Press, 1993). One key difference between confident pluralism and Rawls's political pluralism is the normative value of institutions, which Rawls addressed sporadically and sometimes noncommittally in discussions of the rights of assembly, association, and religion. Confident pluralism's stronger embrace of institutional autonomy (in its commitment to the rights of assembly and association) potentially places it in tension with the Rawlsian project. I thank Larry Solum for insights along these lines.

12 A number of recent works have advanced pluralistic political solutions. See, e.g., Chandran Kukathas, *The Liberal Archipelago: A Theory of Diversity and Freedom* (New York: Oxford University Press, 2003); Nancy L. Rosenblum, *Membership and Morals: The Personal Uses of Pluralism in America* (Princeton, NJ: Princeton University Press, 1998); John Kekes, *The Morality of Pluralism* (Princeton, NJ: Princeton University Press, 1993); Mark E. Warren, *Democracy and Association* (Princeton, NJ: Princeton University Press, 2001); William A. Galston, *Liberal Pluralism: The Implications of Value Pluralism for Political Theory and Practice* (New York: Cambridge University Press, 2002); Victor M. Muniz-Fraticelli, *The Structure of Pluralism* (New York: Oxford University Press, 2014); James W.

Skillen, *Recharging the American Experiment: Principled Pluralism for Genuine Civic Community* (Grand Rapids, MI: Baker Publishing Group, 1994); Jacob T. Levy, *Rationalism, Pluralism, and Freedom* (New York: Oxford University Press, 2015). Confident pluralism draws from some of these insights but does not adopt a previously established theory.

13 Brief of Gays & Lesbians for Individual Liberty as Amicus Curiae in Support of Petitioner at 1, 2, 35, *Christian Legal Soc'y v. Martinez*, 561 U.S. 661 (2010) (No. 08-1371), 2010 WL 530513 (emphasis added); 34 ("It should come as no surprise that GLIL does not agree with CLS's views regarding homosexuality"). Justice Alito's dissent quoted the language of "confident pluralism" from the brief. Christian Legal Society v. Martinez, 561 U.S. 661, 734 (2010) (Alito, J., dissenting). Other gay rights groups weighed in on the opposite side. See, e.g., Brief of Amici Curiae Lambda Legal Defense and Education Fund, Inc., and Gay & Lesbian Advocates & Defenders in Support of Respondents, *Christian Legal Soc'y v. Martinez*, 561 U.S. 661 (2010) (No. 08-1371), 2010 WL 989697.

14 Martha Minow, "Introduction: Robert Cover and Law, Judging, and Violence," in *Narrative, Violence, and the Law: The Essays of Robert Cover*, ed. Martha Minow et al. (Ann Arbor: University of Michigan Press, 1993), 11.

15 Vincent Blasi, "The Pathological Perspective and the First Amendment," *Columbia Law Review* 85, no. 3 (1985): 449, 450–53. See also Jeffrey Stout, *Democracy and Tradition* (Princeton, NJ: Princeton University Press, 2004), 3–15.

16 James Boyd White, *Living Speech: Resisting the Empire of Force* (Princeton, NJ: Princeton University Press, 2006).

CHAPTER 1

1 On the difficulty of identifying a "common good," see, e.g., Bernard Williams, *In the Beginning Was the Deed: Realism and Moralism in Political Argument*, ed. Geoffrey Hawthorn (Princeton, NJ: Princeton University Press, 2008), 29–32; Michael H. v. Gerald D., 491 U.S. 110, 141 (1989) (Brennan, J., dissenting) ("Even if we can agree, therefore, that 'family' and 'parenthood' are part of the good life, it is absurd to assume that we can agree on the content of those terms and destructive to pretend that we do"); Frank Michelman, "Law's Republic," *Yale Law Journal* 97, no. 8 (1988): 1493, 1508 ("In pure pluralist vision, good politics does not essentially involve the direction of reason and argument towards any common, ideal, or self transcendent end"); Cass R. Sunstein, "Interest Groups in American Public Law," *Stanford Law Review* 38, no. 1 (1985): 29, 32–33 ("The pluralist conception treats the republican notion of a separate common good as incoherent, potentially totalitarian, or both").

2 The appeal to shared constitutional commitments locates the argument for confident pluralism within the history and legal structures of the United States. There are, however, aspects of confident pluralism consonant with political and legal responses to deep difference in other jurisdictions. See, e.g., Aernout Nieuwenhuis, "The Concept of Pluralism in the Case-Law of the European Court of Human Rights," *European Constitutional Law Review* 3 (2007): 367. My thanks to Eric Rassbach for bringing this article to my attention.

3 1 Annals of Cong. 457 (Joseph Gales ed., 1834) (remarks of James Madison, June 8,

1789). Madison elsewhere referred to the separation of powers as a "parchment barrier." The Federalist No. 48, at 308 (James Madison) (Clinton Rossiter ed., 1961).

4 Whitney v. California, 274 U.S. 357, 375 (1927) (Brandeis, J., concurring).

5 W. Va. State Bd. of Educ. v. Barnette, 319 U. S. 624, 641–42 (1943).

6 U.S. Const., Amend. I. See generally John D. Inazu, *Liberty's Refuge: The Forgotten Freedom of Assembly* (New Haven, CT: Yale University Press, 2012), 21–25 (discussing reference to Penn).

7 Inazu, *Liberty's Refuge*, 21–25 (describing House debates).

8 Ibid., 28; Irving Brant, *James Madison: Father of the Constitution, 1787–1800* (Indianapolis: Bobbs-Merrill, 1950), 417.

9 Inazu, *Liberty's Refuge*, 26–62; Akhil R. Amar, *The Bill of Rights: Creation and Reconstruction* (New Haven, CT: Yale University Press, 1998), 246.

10 Inazu, *Liberty's Refuge*, 55–58. President Franklin Delano Roosevelt turned to a different formulation of the four freedoms in his 1941 State of the Union address, but the original version heralded assembly.

11 Michael McConnell, "Freedom by Association," *First Things* (August/September 2012), 39, 41. At least one prominent scholar has expressed doubt that the constitutional text (the infinitive "to assemble") encompasses more than the momentary act of gathering. Richard A. Epstein, "Forgotten No More," *Engage* (March 2012), 138 ("For a close textualist, Inazu's most significant maneuver is to transform the constitutional text, which refers to the right of the people to peaceably assemble, into the freedom of assembly, a phrase that, unlike freedom of speech, nowhere appears in the Constitution at all. I believe that this subtle transformation undercuts Inazu's determined effort to make the Assembly Clause the focal point of an expanded right of freedom of association. The two do not map well into each other"). But the verb "assemble" presupposes a noun—an assembly. And while some assemblies occur spontaneously, most do not.

12 Inazu, *Liberty's Refuge*, 45, 47, 188 n.5; Ashutosh Bhagwat, "Associational Speech," *Yale Law Journal* 120 (2011): 978, 998; John Hope Franklin and Alfred A. Moss Jr., *From Slavery to Freedom: A History of African Americans* (New York: McGraw Hill, 1994), 377; Linda J. Lumsden, *Rampant Women: Suffragists and the Right of Assembly* (Knoxville: University of Tennessee Press, 1997), 3; Robert Wuthnow, *Sharing the Journey: Support Groups and America's New Quest for Community* (New York: The Free Press, 1994); Charles Marsh, *The Beloved Community: How Faith Shapes Social Justice, From the Civil Rights Movement to Today* (New York: Basic Books, 2005); Brief of Gays & Lesbians for Individual Liberty as Amicus Curiae in Support of Petitioner at 11, Christian Legal Soc'y v. Martinez, 561 U.S. 661 (2010) (No. 08-1371).

13 Richard W. Garnett, "The Story of Henry Adams's Soul: Education and the Expression of Associations," *Minnesota Law Review* 85 (2001): 1841, 1857; Roberts v. U.S. Jaycees, 468 U.S. 609, 619 (1984). See also Kenneth L. Karst, "The Freedom of Intimate Association," *Yale Law Journal* 89 (1980): 624, 688 ("one of the points of any freedom of association must be to let people make their own definitions of community"); William A. Galston, *Liberal Pluralism: The Implications of Value Pluralism for Political Theory and Practice* (New York: Cambridge University

Press, 2002), 3 ("Liberalism requires a robust though rebuttable presumption in favor of individuals and groups leading their lives as they see fit, within a broad range of legitimate variation, in accordance with their own understanding of what gives life meaning and value").

14 Timothy Zick, "Recovering the Assembly Clause," *Texas Law Review* 91 (2012): 375, 394.

15 Communist Party v. Subversive Activities Control Board, 367 U.S. 1, 137 (1961) (Black J., dissenting).

16 Hillary Rodham Clinton, Address to Carnegie Endowment for Peace, July 30, 2012.

17 See, e.g., Americans Concerned about Religious Freedom, Barna Group (January 18, 2013), https://www.barna.org/barna-update/culture/601-most-americans-are-concerned-about-restrictions-in-religious-freedom (last visited June 1, 2015) (finding that younger Americans are "much less concerned about religious liberty issues").

18 For examples of challenges to government from the religious left, see Jason C. Bivins, *The Fracture of Good Order: Christian Antiliberalism and the Challenge to American Politics* (Chapel Hill: University of North Carolina Press, 2003); Thomas C. Berg, "Progressive Arguments for Religious Organizational Freedom: Reflections on the HHS Mandate," *Journal of Contemporary Legal Issues* 21 (2013): 279, 306.

19 Nelson Tebbe, "Nonbelievers," *Virginia Law Review* 97 (2011): 1111, 1120 (citing studies estimating that between 4 and 5 percent of the population identify as either atheist or agnostic).

20 Town of Greece, NY v. Galloway, 134 S. Ct. 1811 (2014); ibid., slip op. at 23 (Kagan, J., dissenting).

21 Monica Davey and Laurie Goodstein, "Religion Laws Quickly Fall Into Retreat in Indiana and Arkansas," *New York Times*, April 2, 2015 (adding scare quotes to "religious freedom" and "religious liberty"); Corp. of Presiding Bishop of the Church of Jesus Christ of Latter-Day Saints v. Amos, 483 U.S. 327, 345 n.6 (1987) (Brennan, J., concurring) ("It is also conceivable that some for-profit activities could have a religious character, so that religious discrimination with respect to these activities would be justified in some cases").

22 Emp't Div. v. Smith, 494 U.S. 872, 882–90 (1990). See also Church of the Lukumi Babalu Aye, Inc. v. City of Hialeah, 508 U.S. 520, 532–46 (1993) (applying strict scrutiny because challenged ordinances were neither neutral nor generally applicable).

23 Congress enacted the Religious Freedom Restoration Act of 1993 (RFRA), Pub. L. No. 103-141, 107 Stat. 1488, with overwhelming bipartisan support. The Supreme Court held provisions of RFRA as they applied to the states to be unconstitutional in City of Boerne v. Flores, 521 U.S. 507, 536 (1997). See also Michael W. McConnell, John H. Garvey, and Thomas C. Berg, *Religion and the Constitution*, 3rd ed. (New York: Aspen, 2011), 197 (discussing state religious freedom acts enacted after *Smith*); Christopher C. Lund, "Religious Liberty after *Gonzales*: A Look at State RFRAs," *South Dakota Law Review* 55 (2010): 466, 485 ("A surprising number of courts have interpreted state RFRAs to provide less protection than the constitutional clauses they were meant to augment").

24 Burwell v. Hobby Lobby Stores, Inc., No. 13-354 (U.S. June 30, 2014) (applying heightened scrutiny to federal regulation under RFRA); Holt v. Hobbs, No. 13-6827 (U.S. January 20, 2015) (applying heightened scrutiny under section 3 of the Religious Land Use and Institutionalized Persons Act of 2000). For my general skepticism of robust religion-specific constitutional protections in light of *Smith*, see John D. Inazu, "The Freedom of the Church (New Revised Standard Version)," *Journal of Contemporary Legal Issues* 21 (2013): 335; John D. Inazu, "More Is More: Strengthening Free Exercise, Speech, and Association," *Minnesota Law Review* 99 (2014): 485. Others are more optimistic. See, e.g., Richard W. Garnett, "Do Churches Matter? Towards an Institutional Understanding of the Religion Clauses," *Villanova Law Review* 53 (2008): 273; Steven D. Smith, *The Rise and Decline of American Religious Freedom* (Cambridge, MA: Harvard University Press, 2014).

25 Hosanna-Tabor Evangelical Lutheran Church & Sch. v. Equal Emp't Opportunity Comm'n, 132 S. Ct. 694, 710 (2012).

26 See Kenji Yoshino, "The New Equal Protection," *Harvard Law Review* 124 (2011): 747, 748 ("Squeezing law is often like squeezing a balloon. The contents do not escape, but erupt in another area").

27 Inazu, *Liberty's Refuge*, 58–59 (describing Roosevelt's involvement in "Bill of Rights Day" three months prior to his signing Executive Order 9066 authorizing the internment of Japanese Americans).

28 The narrative from Lily Inazu is taken from an interview that I conducted with my grandmother in 1988 (transcript on file with the author). The Supreme Court upheld the internment and related restrictions in Hirabayashi v. United States, 320 U.S. 81 (1943), and Korematsu v. United States, 323 U.S. 214 (1944).

29 Adam Gopnik, "The Caging of America," *New Yorker*, January 30, 2012. See also William J. Stuntz, *The Collapse of American Criminal Justice* (Cambridge, MA: Harvard University Press, 2011); Jed S. Rakoff, "Mass Incarceration: The Silence of the Judges," *New York Review of Books*, May 21, 2015; Sadhbh Walshe, "Expensive and Inhumane: The Shameful State of U.S. Immigrant Detention," *Guardian*, December 3, 2012; Gregory P. Magarian, "Market Triumphalism, Electoral Pathologies, and the Abiding Wisdom of First Amendment Access Rights," *Hofstra Law Review* 35 (2007): 1373, 1423 ("Felon disenfranchisement laws deny the vote to thirteen percent of all black men—1.4 million men who would otherwise be eligible to vote").

30 John D. Inazu, "Let's Talk about Race," *St. Louis Post-Dispatch*, August 14, 2014.

31 See, e.g., Radley Balko, "How Municipalities in St. Louis County, Mo., Profit from Poverty," *Washington Post*, September 3, 2014 (chronicling systemic problems with municipal courts and discussing white paper produced by the St. Louis-based group Arch City Defenders).

32 Brown v. Bd. of Educ., 347 U.S. 483, 493 (1954); McDonnell Douglas Corp. v. Green, 411 U.S. 792, 800 (1973) ("to assure equality . . .").

33 Roberts v. U.S. Jaycees, 468 U.S. 609, 622 (1984); Nancy Rosenblum, *Membership and Morals: The Personal Uses of Pluralism in America* (Princeton, NJ: Princeton University Press, 1988), 36. See also Boy Scouts of America v. Dale, 530 U.S. 640, 647–48 (2000) (finding that freedom of association is "crucial in preventing the

majority from imposing its views on groups that would rather express other, perhaps unpopular, ideas").

34 John Stuart Mill, *On Liberty*, ed. Edward Alexander (Toronto: Broadview Press, 1999), 51–52; United States v. Valle, 301 F.R.D. 53, 60 2014 WL 2980256 (S.D.N.Y. June 30, 2014) (concluding that discussions on Internet chat site about kidnapping, torturing, raping, murdering, and cannibalizing women were "mutual fantasies" and did not constitute intent to carry out the crimes); United States v. Alkhabaz, 104 F.3d 1492 (6th Cir. 1997) (private emails and stories posted to online message boards discussing torturing, raping, and murdering young woman were fantasies that did not constitute criminal threats); Ashcroft v. Free Speech Coalition, 535 U.S. 234 (2002) (invalidating federal law restricting virtual child pornography).

35 Brandenburg v. Ohio, 395 U.S. 444, 449 n.4 (1969).

36 Alasdair MacIntyre, *After Virtue: A Study in Moral Theory*, 3rd ed. (South Bend: University of Notre Dame Press, 2007).

37 Steven D. Smith, "Die and Let Live? The Asymmetry of Accommodation," *Southern California Law Review* 88 (2015): 703, 722. See also Peter Westen, "The Empty Idea of Equality," *Harvard Law Review* 95 (1982): 537.

38 Lawrence B. Joseph, "Some Ways of Thinking about Equality of Opportunity," *Western Political Quarterly* 33 (1980): 393, 399.

39 George Orwell, "Politics and the English Language," *Horizon*, April 1946.

40 For an eloquent description of the inevitably tragic dimension to our aspirations for political community, see Marc O. DeGirolami, *The Tragedy of Religious Freedom* (Cambridge, MA: Harvard University Press, 2013), 3–11.

41 Reinhold Niebuhr, *The Children of Light and the Children of Darkness: A Vindication of Democracy and Critique of Its Traditional Defense* (Chicago: University of Chicago Press, 2011), 118.

CHAPTER 2

1 Prince v. Massachusetts, 321 U.S. 158, 164-65 (1944). The First Amendment contains a sixth right protecting against the establishment of religion. Scholars are divided over whether nonestablishment is a structural or an individual right, but the Supreme Court and popular understandings of the "interwoven" rights of the First Amendment seldom include nonestablishment.

2 See NAACP v. Alabama, 357 U.S. 449 (1958) (recognizing right of association); Christian Legal Society v. Martinez, 561 U.S. 661, 663 (2010) (concluding that right of association claim "merge[s]" with free speech claim).

3 Roberts v. United States Jaycees, 468 U.S. 609, 618, 620 (1984). The Supreme Court recently mentioned the right of intimate association in *Obergefell v. Hodges* 135 S. Ct. 2584 (2015). *Obergefell* incorrectly characterized an earlier case, *Lawrence v. Texas*, 539 U.S. 558 (2004), as relying on intimate association. *Lawrence* overruled *Bowers v. Hardwick*, 478 U.S. 186 (1986). *Bowers* had drawn two dissents, one from Justice Stevens that emphasized substantive due process, and one from Justice Blackmun that drew upon intimate association. *Lawrence* relied on Stevens's dissent and never mentioned intimate association. See Inazu, *Liberty's Refuge*, 135–41.

4 *Roberts*, 618, 622.

5 George Kateb, "The Value of Association," in *Freedom of Association*, ed. Amy Gutmann (Princeton, NJ: Princeton University Press, 1998), 37.

6 http://www.tophatters-mc.com/home.html (last visited June 2, 2015).

7 Gilroy "History," http://www.cityofgilroy.org/cityofgilroy/community/history/default.aspx (last visited June 1, 2015).

8 Villegas v. City of Gilroy, 363 F. Supp. 2d 1207, 12010-11 (N.D. Cal 2005).

9 Ibid., 1217–19; Brief for Appellant at *22, Villegas v. City of Gilroy, 484 F.3d 1136 (9th Cir. 2007) (No. 05-15725) 2005 WL 3128160; Villegas v. City of Gilroy, 484 F.3d 1136 (9th Cir. 2007), *vacated on other grounds sub nom.* by Villegas v. Gilroy Garlic Festival Ass'n, 541 F.3d 950 (9th Cir. 2008) (en banc).

10 http://www.tophatters-mc.com/home.html (last visited June 2, 2015).

11 Ibid.

12 See, e.g., Semaphore Entm't Grp. Sports Corp. v. Gonzalez, 919 F. Supp. 543, 550 n.4 (D.P.R. 1996) (Ultimate Fighting Championship); Cent. Tex. Nudists v. Cnty. of Travis, No. 03-00-00024-CV, 2000 Tex. App. 2000 WL 1784344 at *4 (December 7, 2000) (nudists); Pi Lambda Phi Fraternity, Inc. v. University of Pittsburgh, 229 F.3d 435, 444–47 (3d Cir. 2000) (fraternity); City of Dallas v. Stanglin, 490 U.S. 19, 24–25 (1989) (holding that the patrons of a skating rink were not an expressive association and that "the activity of these dance-hall patrons—coming together to engage in recreational dancing—is not protected by the First Amendment").

13 Ryan Devereaux, "Muslim Student Monitored by the NYPD: 'It Just Brings Everything Home,'" *Guardian*, February 22, 2012; Chris Hawley, "NYPD Monitored Muslim Students All Over the Northeast," Associated Press, February 18, 2012, http://news.yahoo.com/nypd-monitored-muslim-students-over-northeast-201653480.html; "New York Police Monitored Muslim Students at Rutgers University, Other Colleges," Associated Press, February 19, 2012, http://www.nj.com/news/index.ssf/2012/02/new_york_police_monitored_musl.html.

14 Devereaux, "Muslim Student Monitored by the NYPD."

15 Hawley, "NYPD Monitored Muslim Students"; Yasmin Gagne, "AP: NYPD Monitored Columbia's Muslim Student's Association," *Columbia Spectator*, February 18, 2012; Diala Shamas and Nermeen Arastu, "Mapping Muslims: NYPD Spying and Its Impact on American Muslims" (2013), 40, http://www.law.cuny.edu/academics/clinics/immigration/clear/Mapping-Muslims.pdf.

16 Devereaux, "Muslim Student Monitored by the NYPD" ("Please refrain from"); Shamas and Arastu, "Mapping Muslims," 14, 20, 40 ("American Muslim interviewees," and "the NYPD's surveillance"); Conor Friedersdorf, "The Horrifying Effects of NYPD Ethnic Profiling on Innocent Muslim Americans," *The Atlantic*, March 28, 2013, http://www.theatlantic.com/politics/archive/2013/03/the-horrifying-effects-of-nypd-ethnic-profiling-on-innocent-muslim-americans/274434/ ("The students wouldn't come").

17 Matt Apuzzo and Joseph Goldstein, "New York Drops Unit That Spied on Muslims," *New York Times*, April 15, 2014; Yasemin Akcaguner, "After NYPD Surveillance Unit Disbands, Students Want Admins to Reaffirm Privacy Protection," *Columbia Spectator*, April 18, 2014.

18 Neil M. Richards, "The Dangers of Surveillance," *Harvard Law Review* 126 (2013): 1934, 1951.

19 NAACP v. Alabama, 357 U.S. 449 (1958) (recognizing a constitutional right of association); Inazu, *Liberty's Refuge*, 63–96 (discussing early history of association right); Harry Kalven Jr., *A Worthy Tradition: Freedom of Speech in America* ed. Jamie Kalven (New York: Harper and Row, 1988), 259.

20 Roberts v. United States Jaycees, 468 U.S. 609, 613 (1984); United States Jaycees v. McClure, 709 F.2d 1560, 1563 (8th Cir. 1983).

21 *Roberts*, 614–16.

22 Brief for Appellee at 14, 20–21, *Roberts v. United States Jaycees* (March 22, 1984).

23 *Roberts*, 623, 626.

24 Ibid., 623.

25 Boy Scouts of America v. Dale, 530 U.S. 640 (2000).

26 Ibid., 651. For another scholar expressing skepticism about the traction of the *Boy Scouts* decision, see Richard A. Epstein, "The Constitutional Perils of Moderation: The Case of the Boy Scouts," *Southern California Law Review* 74 (2000): 119, 122. See also Every Nation Campus Ministries at San Diego State Univ. v. Achtenberg, 597 F.Supp.2d 1075, 1083 (S.D. Cal. 2009) ("state action that burdens a group's ability to engage in expressive association [need not] always be subject to strict scrutiny") (quoting Truth v. Kent Sch. Dist. 542 F.3d 634, 652 (9th Cir. 2008) (Fisher, J., concurring)); Chi Iota Colony of Alpha Epsilon Pi Fraternity v. City Univ. of N.Y., 502 F.3d 136, 139 (2d Cir. 2007) ("The mere fact that the associational interest asserted is recognized by the First Amendment does not necessarily mean that a regulation which burdens that interest must satisfy strict scrutiny"). For commentators who view the *Boy Scouts* case more favorably, see, e.g., Seana Valentine Shiffrin, "What Is Really Wrong with Compelled Association?," *Northwestern University Law Review* 99 (2005): 839; Dale Carpenter, "Expressive Association and Anti-Discrimination Law after *Dale*: A Tripartite Approach," *Minnesota Law Review* 85 (2001): 1515, 1532–33.

27 *Boy Scouts*, 679 (Stevens, J., dissenting); Andrew Koppelman with Tobias Barrington Wolff, *A Right to Discriminate?: How the Case of* Boy Scouts of America v. James Dale *Warped the Law of Free Association* (New Haven, CT: Yale University Press, 2009).

28 See Gay Students Org. of the Univ. of N.H. v. Bonner, 509 F.2d 652, 661 (1st Cir. 1974) (upholding associational rights of a gay student group); Brief for Petitioner at 30, *Christian Legal Society v. Martinez*, 561 U.S. 661 (2010) (No. 08-1371), 2010 WL 711183 2; Carpenter, "Expressive Association and Anti-Discrimination Law after *Dale*," 1515, 1532–33. See also Lawrence A. Wilson and Rafael Shannon, "Homosexual Organizations and the Right of Association," *Hastings Law Journal* 30 (1979): 1029, 1046–62; One Eleven Wines & Liquors Inc. v. Div. of Alcoholic Beverage Control, 235 A.2d 12, 19 (N.J. 1967) (upholding rights of gays to congregate in bars).

29 Carpenter, "Expressive Association and Anti-Discrimination Law after *Dale*," 1550–51.

30 Roberts v. United States Jaycees, 468 U.S. 609, 618 (1984) ("associate for the purpose . . .") (emphasis added); Emp't Div. v. Smith, 494 U.S. 872, 882–91 (1990).

31 Christian Legal Society v. Martinez, 561 U.S. 661, 680 (2010).

32 Hosanna-Tabor Evangelical Lutheran Church & Sch. v. EEOC, 132 S. Ct. 694 (2012). See also 42 U.S.C. § 2000e, et seq.; Corporation of the Presiding Bishop of

the Church of Jesus Christ of Latter-Day Saints v. Amos, 483 U.S. 327 (1987); Conlon v. InterVarsity Christian Fellowship, 777 F.3d 829 (6th Cir. 2015).

33 Truth v. Kent. Sch. Dist., 542 F.3d 634, 645 (9th Cir. 2008); Alpha Delta Chi–Delta Chapter v. Reed, 648 F.3d 790, 795–96 (9th Cir. 2011).

34 See John D. Inazu, "The Four Freedoms and the Future of Religious Liberty," *North Carolina Law Review* 92 (2014): 787, 793 n. 20.

35 Manny Fernandez et al., "9 Are Killed in Biker Gang Shootout in Waco," *New York Times*, May 17, 2015.

CHAPTER 3

1 See, e.g., Widmar v. Vincent, 454 U.S. 263, 267–70 (1981) (recognizing public university facilities generally open to students are public forums). The public forum doctrine can be traced to Hague v. Comm. for Indus. Org., 307 U.S. 496, 514–16 (1939). See generally John D. Inazu, "The First Amendment's Public Forum," *William & Mary Law Review* 56 (2015): 1159.

2 Perry Education Association v. Perry Local Educators' Association, 460 U.S. 37, 45 (1983). In limited public forums, "the State is not required to and does not allow persons to engage in every type of speech," and "the State may be justified in 'reserving [its forum] for certain groups or for the discussion of certain topics.'" Good News Club v. Milford Cent. Sch., 533 U.S. 98, 106 (2001).

3 Diana L. Eck, "The Challenge of Pluralism," *Nieman Reports* 47, no. 2 (Summer 1993); *Perry Education Association*, 45 (noting that streets and parks are "quintessential public forums"). As Robert Post has observed, *Perry*'s assertion that the government's regulatory authority in a limited public forum is "bound by the same standards as apply in a traditional public forum" ignores the fact that government can restrict both content and the class of speakers in a limited public forum. Robert C. Post, "Between Governance and Management: The History and Theory of the Public Forum," *UCLA Law Review* 34 (1987): 1713, 1753.

4 *Parks & Recreation*, season 4, episode 4 ("Pawnee Ranger").

5 Boos v. Barry, 485 U.S. 312, 318 (1988) (quoting New York Times Co. v. Sullivan, 376 U.S. 254, 270 [1964]) ("uninhibited, robust, and wide-open").

6 *Parks & Recreation*, season 2, episode 5 ("Sister City").

7 Harrison Jacobs, "Missouri Police Fire Tear Gas at TV Crew and Take Their Equipment," *Business Insider*, August 14, 2014; Paul Szoldra, "SWAT Team Called on Peaceful Protesters in Ferguson—Police Arrest Journalists, Fire Tear Gas and Rubber Bullets," *Business Insider*, August 13, 2014.

8 See Timothy Zick, *Speech Out of Doors: Preserving First Amendment Liberties in Public Places* (New York: Cambridge University Press, 2009), 223–42, 277–81 ("free speech zones"); John D. Inazu and Marion Crain, "Re-Assembling Labor," *Illinois Law Review* (2015): 1791 (restrictions on labor protests); Jeremy Kessler, "The Closing of the Public Square," *New Republic*, January 12, 2012 (restrictions against Occupy protesters); Hill v. Colorado, 530 U.S. 703 (2000) (restrictions against antiabortion protesters).

9 Martin Luther King Jr., "I've Been to the Mountaintop," April 3, 1968.

10 See Brown v. Entm't Merch. Ass'n, 131 S. Ct. 2729 (2011) (striking down California regulation on the sale of violent video games that included scenes of simulated rape and torture); United States v. Alvarez, 132 S. Ct. 2537 (2012) (striking down

Stolen Valor Act that prohibited lying about military service decorations); United States v. Stevens, 559 U.S. 460 (2010) (striking down regulations aimed at sexual fetishes involving the torture and killing of animals).

11 Ward v. Rock Against Racism, 491 U.S. 781, 791, 809 (1989).

12 See Rosenberger v. Rector & Visitors of Univ. of Va., 515 U.S. 819, 830–31 (1995) ("Discrimination against one set of views or ideas is but a subset or particular instance of the more general phenomenon of content discrimination. And, it must be acknowledged, the distinction is not a precise one"). The meaning of the content neutrality doctrine is far from clear—as law professor Steven Shiffrin has quipped, "if content neutrality is the First Amendment emperor, the emperor has no clothes." Steven H. Shiffrin, *Dissent, Injustice, and the Meanings of America* (Princeton, NJ: Princeton University Press, 1999), 66.

13 *Ward*, 791 ("leave open ample . . ."); Bay Area Peace Navy v. United States, 914 F.2d 1224, 1229 (9th Cir. 1990) ("intended audience"); Serv. Emp. Int'l Union v. City of Los Angeles, 114 F. Supp.2d 966, 972 (C.D. Cal. 2000) ("sharpest eyesight"); Marcavage v. City of New York, 689 F.3d 98, 107–8 (2d Cir. 2012) (rejecting argument that being within "sight and sound" is a constitutionally required condition of an ample alternative channel).

14 *Hill*, 726 and 781 (Kennedy, J., dissenting); Riley v. Nat'l Fed'n of the Blind of N. Carolina, Inc., 487 U.S. 781, 791 (1988). See also Schneider v. State of N.J. (Town of Irvington), 308 U.S. 147, 163 (1939) ("One is not to have the exercise of his liberty of expression in appropriate places abridged on the plea that it may be exercised in some other place").

15 Zick, *Speech Out of Doors*, 21; Timothy Zick, "Recovering the Assembly Clause," *Texas Law Review* 91 (2012): 375, 396. See also City of Renton v. Playtime Theatres, Inc., 475 U.S. 41, 64 (1986) (Brennan, J., dissenting) (observing that city ordinance upheld by majority under time, place, and manner analysis rendered 95% of city land unavailable for adult business).

16 City Council v. Taxpayers for Vincent, 466 U.S. 789, 820 (1984) (Brennan, J., dissenting) (quoting *Martin v. Struthers*, 319 U.S. 141, 146 (1943)).

17 Public forum analysis is further complicated by the Supreme Court's distinctions between traditional, limited, and nonpublic forums. The bulk of the examples that I highlight in this chapter are either traditional or limited public forums whose form or function is consonant with what Dean Robert Post calls "governance" forums, in which "the state is bound by the ordinary principles of First Amendment jurisprudence." Post, "Between Governance and Management," 1775.

18 Pleasant Grove City v. Summum, 555 U.S. 460 (2009). See also Locke v. Davey, 540 U.S. 712, 720 n.3 (2004) (holding that a state-run scholarship program is not a "forum for speech"); Cornelius v. NAACP Legal Def. & Educ. Fund, Inc., 473 U.S. 788, 806 (1985) (holding that a federal workplace charitable fundraising campaign is a nonpublic forum).

19 *Parks & Recreation*, season 2, episode 24 ("Freddy Spaghetti"); See Eugene Volokh, "Freedom of Expressive Association and Government Subsidies," *Stanford Law Review* 58 (2006): 1919, 1940.

20 Cox v. Louisiana, 379 U.S. 536, 554–55 (1965).

21 Baylen J. Linnekin, "'Tavern Talk' and the Origins of the Assembly Clause: Trac-

ing the First Amendment's Assembly Clause Back to Its Roots in Colonial Taverns," *Hastings Constitutional Law Quarterly* 39 (2012): 593, 596; Peter Thompson, *Rum, Punch, and Revolution* (Philadelphia: University of Pennsylvania Press, 1999), 16–17.

22 William N. Eskridge Jr., "Challenging the Apartheid of the Closet: Establishing Conditions for Lesbian and Gay Intimacy, Nomos, and Citizenship, 1961–1981," *Hofstra Law Review* 25 (1997): 817, 822 (describing the significance of the Stonewall riots); Neil Tesser, "Amazingrace," *Northwestern Magazine* (Fall 2011), http://www.northwestern.edu/magazine/fall2011/feature/amazingrace.html; Darryl Pinckney, "In Ferguson," *New York Review of Books*, January 8, 2015.

23 Lisa W. Foderaro, "Privately Owned Park, Open to the Public, May Make Its Own Rules," *New York Times*, October 13, 2011; Colin Moynihan, "Park Gives Wall St. Protesters a Place to Call Home," *New York Times*, September 27, 2011.

24 James Barron and Colin Moynihan, "City Reopens Park After Protesters Are Evicted," *New York Times*, November 15, 2011; Mattathias Schwartz, "Pre-Occupied: The Origins and Future of Occupy Wall Street," *New Yorker*, November 28, 2011; Waller v. City of New York, 34 Misc. 3d 371, 375 (N.Y. Sup. Ct. 2011) ("The owner has the right to adopt reasonable rules that permit it to maintain a clean, safe, publicly accessible space consonant with the responsibility it assumed to provide public access according to law"); People v. Nunez, 36 Misc.3d 172, 181–83 (N.Y. Crim. Ct. 2012) (rejecting First Amendment defense to criminal trespass law by Occupier who refused to leave Zuccotti Park).

25 Gregory P. Magarian, "The First Amendment, the Public-Private Distinction, and Nongovernmental Suppression of Wartime Political Debate," *George Washington University Law Review* 73 (2004): 101, 133. For a defense of the state action distinction between public and private, see Lillian BeVier & John Harrison, "The State Action Principle and Its Critics," *Virginia Law Review* 96 (2010): 1767.

26 Amalgamated Food Emp. Union Local 590 v. Logan Valley Plaza, Inc., 391 U.S. 308 (1968), and 332 (Black, J., dissenting); Lloyd Corp. v. Tanner, 407 U.S. 551 (1972); Pruneyard Shopping Ctr. v. Robins, 447 U.S. 74 (1980). See also Hudgens v. NLRB, 424 U.S. 507, 518 (1976) (overruling *Logan Valley*).

27 Zick, *Speech Out of Doors*, 144–47.

28 Mark A. Lemley, "Place and Cyberspace," *California Law Review* 91 (2003): 521, 535.

29 Lyrissa Lidsky, "Public Forum 2.0," *Boston University Law Review* 91 (2011): 1975, 1996–2002.

30 "Nation of Islam," *Twitter*, https://twitter.com/officialnoi (last visited June 2, 2015); Jeff Fleischer, "Nation of Islam Women Look Up and Out," Womensnews .org, August 2, 2005, http://womensenews.org/story/religion/050802/nation -islam-women-look-and-out; Donaldson v. Farrakhan, 762 N.E.2d 835 (Mass. 2002) (upholding First Amendment right of Nation of Islam to exclude women from a male-only meeting in a city-owned theater).

31 Some of the few offline examples of voluntary groups nested within more regulated commercial actors include forums of student organizations or alumni groups at for-profit universities (relative outliers in higher education) and sports fan clubs licensed and facilitated by professional sports teams.

32 Dawn C. Nunziato, "The Death of the Public Forum in Cyberspace," *Berkeley Technology Law Journal* 20 (2005): 1115, 1117, 1132.

33 Jerome A. Barron, "Access to the Press—A New First Amendment Right," *Harvard Law Review* 80 (1967): 1641, 1641, 1649. The legal and policy questions posed by mass media are related to but distinct from the questions raised by private public forums. See, e.g., Red Lion Broad. Co. v. FCC, 395 U.S. 367, 386–90 (upholding broadcast access regulation based on scarcity of broadcast spectrum); Turner Broad. Sys., Inc. v. FCC, 512 U.S. 622, 637–40 (1994) (distinguishing *Red Lion*'s scarcity argument in context of cable television access).

34 Civil Rights Act of 1964, 42 U.S.C. §§ 2000a(b), (e) (2006). See also Joseph William Singer, "No Right to Exclude: Public Accommodations and Private Property," *Northwestern University Law Review* 90 (1996): 1283. The cases characterizing groups as public accommodations are *Boy Scouts of America v. Dale*, 530 U.S. 640, 656–57 (2000) (characterizing the Boy Scouts as a place of public accommodation under New Jersey law) and *Roberts v. United States Jaycees*, 468 U.S. 609, 625–26 (1984) (characterizing the Jaycees as a place of public accommodation under Minnesota law).

35 *Parks & Recreation*, season 4, episode 4 ("Pawnee Rangers").

36 Harry Kalven Jr., "The Concept of the Public Forum: *Cox v. Louisiana*," *Supreme Court Review* 1965 (1965): 1, 8, 12.

CHAPTER 4

1 Bob Jones University v. United States, 461 U.S. 574, 580–81 (1983).

2 See, e.g., Rust v. Sullivan, 500 U.S. 173, 199–200 (1991) (referring to "the existence of a Government 'subsidy,' in the form of Government-owned property . . . open to the public for expressive activity."). For scholars who distinguish between facilitating and funding, see, e.g., Corey Brettschneider, *When the State Speaks, What Should It Say?: How Democracies Can Protect Expression and Promote Equality* (Princeton, NJ: Princeton University Press, 2012), 4, 9; Susan Frelich Appleton, "Liberty's Forgotten Refugees? Engendering Assembly," *Washington University Law Review* 89 (2012): 1423, 1426.

3 See 26 U.S.C. § 170(c) (2006) (authorizing deductions); 26 U.S.C. § 501(c)(3) (2006) (specifying which tax-exempt organizations are eligible to receive deductions).

4 The federal tax code recognizes tax-exempt organizations formed "for religious, charitable, scientific, literary, or educational purposes." 26 U.S.C. § 170(c)(2)(B) (2006).

5 Tex. Monthly, Inc. v. Bullock, 489 U.S. 1, 14 (1989); Regan v. Taxation with Representation of Wash., 461 U.S. 540, 544 (1983); John D. Colombo and Mark A. Hall, *The Charitable Tax Exemption* (Boulder, CO: Westview Press, 1995), 155. See also Saul Levmore, "Taxes as Ballots," *University of Chicago Law Review* 65 (1998): 387, 405.

6 See John D. Inazu, "A Confident Pluralism," *Southern California Law Review* 88 (2015): 587, 611 n.98 (citing IRC provisions and IRS regulations), 612 n.100 (citing websites of tax-exempt organizations).

7 The nature of the tax exemption under § 501(c)(3) is traceable to the traditional

law of charitable trusts. See James J. Fishman & Stephen Schwarz, *Nonprofit Organizations* (New York: Foundation Press, 1995), 28–38. It stands in contrast to a "managerial domain" of government. See Robert C. Post, "Subsidized Speech," *Yale Law Journal* 106 (1996): 151, 164.

8 Pub. L. No. 94-439, § 209, 90 Stat. 1418, 1434 (1976). The Supreme Court has concluded that the First Amendment does not require the neutral dispersal of discretionary grants and contracts to private groups. See, e.g., Harris v. McRae, 448 U.S. 297 (1980); Nat'l Endowment for the Arts v. Finley, 524 U.S. 569, 572–73 (1998). But see Agency for Int'l Dev. v. Alliance for Open Soc'y Int'l, Inc., 133 S. Ct. 2321, 2330 (2013); Legal Servs. Corp. v. Velazquez, 531 U.S. 533, 536–40 (2001).

9 Rosenberger v. Rector & Visitors of Univ. of Va., 515 U.S. 819, 823, 834 (1995).

10 Brettschneider, *When the State Speaks*, 44, 138. Similar reasoning explains why "official recognition" of the Christian group in *Christian Legal Society v. Martinez* did not signal any endorsement of the group's views by the law school. See Brief for Petitioner at 4, *Christian Legal Soc'y v. Martinez*, 561 U.S. 661 (No. 08-1371) (2010) (noting that Hastings College of the Law made clear that it "neither sponsor[ed] nor endorse[d]" officially recognized groups and insisted that those groups inform third parties that they were not sponsored by the law school).

11 *Big Mama Rag* 1, no. 1 (October 1972): 1; Roseanne Barr, *Roseannearchy: Dispatches from the Nut Farm* (New York: Gallery Books, 2011), 111. See also Elissa Meyer, "*Big Mama Rag* Born Out of Frustration, Success," *Big Mama Rag* 2, no. 7 (May 1974): 2 ("*Big Mama Rag* was born out of the need for expression, women's expression").

12 "Where We're At," *Big Mama Rag* 1, no. 1 (October 1972): 10 ("quite a struggle"); Brief For Appellants, 6 (citing App 68) ("over two-thirds . . .").

13 *Big Mama Rag* 2, no. 1 (April 1974): 1; Linda Fowler, "BMR: Where We're At," *Big Mama Rag* 3, no. 3 (September 1974): 5.

14 *Big Mama Rag* 3, no. 4 (October 1974): 1; Big Mama Rag, Inc. v. United States, 631 F.2d 1030, 1032–33 (1980). According to the officials, these views represented an "unwritten policy" of the IRS.

15 Maureen Mrizek, "What Does the Word Lesbian Do to You?" *Big Mama Rag* 1, no. 1 (October 1972); *Big Mama Rag* 1, no. 5 (October/November 1973).

16 "BMR, Lambda Question Unwritten Rule: IRS Denies Tax Exemption" *Big Mama Rag* 4, no. 10 (November 1976): 5. The IRS issued a final decision upholding the denial of tax-exempt status in June 1977. Brief for Appellees, Big Mama Rag, Inc. v. United States, No. 79-1826 (Dec. 11, 1979): 10–11 (citing IRS letter dated June 24, 1977). That final decision meant that *Big Mama* had exhausted its efforts to reach a favorable decision within the IRS and could now take its case to federal court.

17 Big Mama Rag, Inc. v. United States, 494 F. Supp. 473 (1979); "Sirica Rules Against BMR," *Big Mama Rag* 7 no. 5 (June 1979): 26. Although the court rejected most of *Big Mama*'s claims, it found the IRS's argument that *Big Mama* failed to qualify for tax-exempt status "because it does not instruct the public on subjects useful to the community" a standard that was "far too subjective in its application to pass constitutional muster." *Big Mama Rag*, 479 n. 6.

18 Brief for Appellants, Big Mama Rag, Inc. v. United States, No. 79-1826 (October 11, 1979): 7, 8.

19 "Six Years in Court," *Big Mama Rag* 8, no. 9 (October 1980): 1; Big Mama Rag, Inc. v. United States, 631 F.2d 1030, 1034 (D.C. Cir. 1980). The holding rests on the vagueness of the IRS's definition of "educational," but the underlying pluralist rationales are also evident in the opinion.

20 "BMR: Where We're At," *Big Mama Rag* 10, no. 2 (February 1982): 2 ("winning a federal . . ."); *Big Mama Rag* 12, no. 4 (April 1984): 2 ("Last issue . . .").

21 Bob Jones Univ. v. United States, 461 U.S. 574, 580–81 (1983). My mom is a Midwesterner with German and English roots. Dad is Japanese. Mom graduated from the University of Kansas in 1968; Dad's degree is from Rutgers in 1965—they met after college. But it's pretty clear that Bob Jones would not have approved of their courtship and marriage (or their offspring).

22 I.R.S. Rev. Rul. 71-447 2 (1971); Bob Jones Univ. v. United States, 468 F.Supp. 890, 893 (D.S.C. 1978); Goldsboro Christian Schs., Inc. v. United States, 436 F.Supp. 1314, 1317 (E.D.N.C. 1977). Both schools maintained racially discriminatory policies based on their interpretations of the Bible.

23 Bob Jones Univ. v. United States, 461 U.S. 574, 592, 595 (1983); Olatunde Johnson, "The Story of *Bob Jones University v. United States*: Race, Religion, and Congress' Extraordinary Acquiescence," in *Statutory Interpretation Stories*, ed. William N. Eskridge Jr. et al. (New York: Foundation Press, 2011), 155; Mayer G. Freed and Daniel D. Polsby, "Race, Religion, and Public Policy: *Bob Jones University v. United States*," *Supreme Court Review* (1983): 1, 2 ("it is a mistake . . .").

24 *Bob Jones University*, 609 (Powell, J., concurring) ("Far from representing . . ."). See also Miranda Perry Fleischer, "Theorizing the Charitable Tax Subsidies: The Role of Distributive Justice," *Washington University Law Review* 87 (2010): 505, 513 ("As a general rule, such organizations must provide some type of 'community benefit' in the form of fulfilling needs unmet by the private market. Precisely what counts as a community benefit, however, is unclear"); Miriam Galston, "Public Policy Constraints on Charitable Organizations," *Virginia Tax Review* 3 (1984): 291, 292 ("[T]he Supreme Court has misread the common law of charity into the Code while confusing the public policy and public benefit strands of charitable trust law").

25 The context of *Bob Jones* may help explain some of the other rare instances in which federal courts have upheld the denial of tax-exempt status to organizations claiming to be "educational" or "charitable" under the Internal Revenue Code. For example, the same court that ruled in favor of *Big Mama* in 1980 three years later denied tax-exempt status to a white supremacist organization. See *Nat'l Alliance v. United States*, 710 F.2d 868 (D.C. Cir. 1983). See also *Nationalist Movement v. Commissioner*, 37 F.3d 216, 220 (5th Cir. 1994) (upholding as not "clearly erroneous" the Tax Court's determination that the Nationalist Movement's counseling services were "not exclusively charitable in nature"). Outside of cases involving racial animus, most limitations on tax-exempt status involve organizations deemed to be manipulating the tax system itself. See, e.g., *The Ecclesiastical Order of the Ism of Am, Inc. v. Commissioner*, 80 T.C. 833, 843 (1983) (denying tax-exempt status to organization devoted to what the court characterized as "tax information and advice as to methods of tax avoidance, if not downright tax evasion"); *Hernandez v. Commissioner*, 490 U.S. 680 (1989) (deny-

ing tax-exempt status to Church of Scientology because Court concluded that each contribution amounted to a "quid pro quo" for taxpayers).

26 Eugene Volokh, "Freedom of Expressive Association and Government Subsidies," *Stanford Law Review* 58 (2006): 1919, 1963; Jeff Spinner-Halev, "A Restrained View of Transformation," *Political Theory* 39 (2011): 777, 782; Douglas Laycock, "Tax Exemptions for Racially Discriminatory Religious Schools," *Texas Law Review* 60 (1982): 259, 276.

27 Doe v. Kamehameha Schs./Bernice Pauahi Bishop Estate, 470 F.3d 827, 829 (9th Cir. 2006) (en banc) (upholding private school's Hawaiian-only admissions policy against a § 1981 challenge).

28 On gender discrimination, see United States v. Virginia, 518 U.S. 515 (1996) (holding that Virginia's all-male military academy violated the Equal Protection Clause); Richard Schmalbeck and Lawrence Zelenak, *Federal Income Taxation*, 2nd ed. (New York: Aspen, 2007), 469 n. 5 (discussing the contrast between the IRS's treatment of racially discriminatory and single-sex colleges).

29 *Obergefell v. Hodges*, No. 14-556 (April 28, 2015), Oral Argument Transcript, p. 38; Mark Oppenheimer, "Now's the Time To End Tax Exemptions for Religious Institutions," *Time*, June 28, 2015.

30 See Mario L. Barnes, Erwin Chemerinsky, and Trina Jones, "A Post-Race Equal Protection?," *Georgetown Law Journal* 98 (2010): 967, 972 ("[T]he history, social reality, and life circumstances of people of color in this country do not support a broad adoption of the post-racial perspective within equal protection analysis"). For examples of the extraordinary restrictions imposed on private groups and individuals in furtherance of ending racial discrimination against African Americans, see Shelley v. Kraemer, 334 U.S. 1 (1948) (striking down racially restrictive real estate covenants); Jones v. Alfred H. Mayer Co., 392 U.S. 409 (1968) (barring racial discrimination in the sale or lease of private property); Sullivan v. Little Hunting Park, Inc., 396 U.S. 229 (1969) (extending *Jones* to membership in a community park and playground); Tillman v. Wheaton-Haven Recreation Ass'n, 410 U.S. 431 (1973) (extending *Jones* to a private swimming pool); Norwood v. Harrison, 413 U.S. 455, 463 (1973) (upholding denial of state-funded textbook loans to students attending racially discriminatory private schools); Runyon v. McCrary, 427 U.S. 160, 168 (1976) (barring racial discrimination by "private, commercially operated, nonsectarian schools").

31 Robert M. Cover, "The Supreme Court, 1982 Term—Foreword: Nomos and Narrative," *Harvard Law Review* 97 (1983): 4.

32 Ibid., 44; Allen v. Wright, 468 U.S. 737, 785, 788 (1984) (Stevens, J., dissenting).

33 Cover, "Nomos and Narrative," 28; Minow, "Introduction," 1–2, 7.

34 Colombo and Hall, *The Charitable Tax Exemption*, 155; Walz v. Tax Comm'n of City of New York, 397 U.S. 664, 689 (1970) (Brennan, J., concurring) (referring specifically to religious nonprofits). Justice Rehnquist's dissent in *Bob Jones* emphasized a separate reason for upholding the tax-exemption to the university: the disjunction between "charitable" and "educational" in the Internal Revenue Code. *Bob Jones University*, 623 (Rehnquist, J., dissenting) (noting that the university clearly qualified as an "educational" organization).

35 Other areas of the law have fared better. One example is a federal law known as

the Equal Access Act, 20 U.S.C. § 4071–4074. The law compels federally funded secondary schools to provide equal access to their facilities for extracurricular clubs. Since its enactment in 1984, the Equal Access Act has been used to ensure access for conservative religious groups and gay-straight alliances. It has been enlisted in progressive school districts on behalf of conservative Christians, and in conservative school districts on behalf of Muslim, Jewish, Sikh, and nonreligious groups. See Michael W. McConnell et al., *Religion and the Constitution* (New York: Wolters Kluwer, 2011), 678 ("The Act protects political and philosophical as well as religious groups. One of the principal nonreligious applications of the Act has been to permit students to form gay rights clubs").

CHAPTER 5

1 "Chicago Dave," email (August 21, 2014) (on file with author).

2 John D. Inazu, "Are We Ferguson?" *CNN*, August 22, 2014, http://www.cnn.com /2014/08/21/opinion/inazu-ferguson-race-class-brown/.

3 The Internet adage is usually attributed to Mike Godwin, "Meme, Countermeme," *Wired* (October 1994), http://archive.wired.com/wired/archive/2.10/god win.if_pr.html.

4 Cass R. Sunstein, *Republic.com 2.0* (Princeton, NJ: Princeton University Press, 2009), 76–78.

5 The Sandy Principle may also reinforce "way-of-life" divisions based on race, class, and politics. See Joseph Bottom, *An Anxious Age: The Post-Protestant Ethic and the Spirit of America* (New York: Crown Publishing, 2014), 29–30.

6 John Stuart Mill, *On Liberty*, ed. Edward Alexander (Toronto: Broadview Press, 1999), 62.

7 Michael H. v. Gerald D., 491 U.S. 110, 141 (1989) (Brennan, J., dissenting).

8 Charles Taylor, "Conditions of an Unforced Consensus on Human Rights," in *Dilemmas and Connections* (Cambridge, MA: Belknap Press, 2011), 105. The intuition for a thinly held agreement bears obvious resemblance to John Rawls's "overlapping consensus." See John Rawls, *Political Liberalism* (New York: Columbia University Press, 1993); see also Rebecca L. Brown, "Common Good and Common Ground: The Inevitability of Fundamental Disagreement," *University of Chicago Law Review* 81 (2014): 397, 399 (the terrain of Rawls's overlapping consensus "must remain quite thin").

9 The character meme draws from Alasdair MacIntyre, *After Virtue: A Study in Moral Theory*, 3rd. ed. (South Bend: University of Notre Dame Press, 2007). The "Conservative Moralist" is taken from MacIntyre's prologue to the third edition (xv).

10 Bernard Williams, "Toleration: An Impossible Virtue?" in *Toleration: An Elusive Virtue*, ed. David Heyd (Princeton, NJ: Princeton University Press, 1996), 18.

11 Edward Langerak, *Civil Disagreement: Personal Integrity in a Pluralistic Society* (Washington, DC: Georgetown University Press, 2014), 78.

12 Simon Blackburn, "Religion and Respect," in *Philosophers without Gods: Meditations on Atheism and the Secular Life*, ed. Louise M. Antony (Oxford: Oxford University Press, 2007), 180, quoted in Brian Leiter, *Why Tolerate Religion?* (Princeton, NJ: Princeton University Press, 2013), 74–75.

13 Leslie Newbigin, *Proper Confidence: Faith, Doubt, and Certainty in Christian Discipleship* (Grand Rapids, MI: Eerdmans, 1995), 102.

14 Diana Eck, "What Is Pluralism?" available at http://pluralism.org/pluralism/what _is_pluralism (last visited June 2, 2015). For an explanation of why pluralism is not relativism, see William E. Connolly, *Pluralism* (Durham, NC: Duke University Press, 2005).

15 Sacks, *The Dignity of Difference*, 23; Haidt, *The Righteous Mind*, 58. See also Martha Minow, "Should Religious Groups Be Exempt from Civil Rights Laws?," *Boston College Law Review* 48 (2007): 781, 844 ("Might a gesture of humility offer a thread of commonality even between religious people confident of their faith and civil rights advocates and enforcers, confident of theirs?").

16 See, e.g., Rebecca Tushnet, "Judges as Bad Reviewers: Fair Use and Epistemological Humility," *Law & Literature* 25 (2013): 20, 29 (suggesting that judges should adopt "a kind of epistemological humility" in evaluating fair use claims in copyright). The possibility of embracing this version of humility is one reason that I have focused on "aspirations" rather than "virtues." Tolerance, humility, and patience are also virtues, but virtues emerge out of traditions and practices that presume a degree of coherence and continuity. See, e.g., MacIntyre, *After Virtue*. At some point the traditions and practices sustaining virtues may simply be incompatible. If we have reached that point in our society—and perhaps we have—then an appeal to shared virtues asks too much. Aspirations aim for something less ambitious, and they may require far less agreement to cohere across disparate traditions.

17 The details in this section draw from Rodney A. Smolla, *Jerry Falwell v. Larry Flynt: The First Amendment on Trial* (New York: St. Martin's Press, 1988), and Larry Flynt, "My Friend, Jerry Falwell," *Los Angeles Times*, May 20, 2007.

18 Bill Forman, "Candidates of the Week: Hustler's Larry Flynt vs. Porn Actress Mary Carey," *Sacramento News and Review*, August 14, 2003; Marc Ambinder, "Falwell Suggests Gays to Blame for Attacks," *ABC News*, September 14, 2011 (quoting Falwell), http://abcnews.go.com/Politics/story?id=121322.

19 Flynt, "My Friend, Jerry Falwell"; Smolla, *Jerry Falwell v. Larry Flynt*, appendix I.

20 Hustler Magazine, Inc. v. Falwell, 485 U.S. 46 (1988); Mary Battiata, "'Felt Like Weeping,' Falwell Tells Jurors," *Washington Post*, December 5, 1984.

CHAPTER 6

1 See Frederick Schauer, "The Boundaries of the First Amendment: A Preliminary Exploration of Constitutional Salience," *Harvard Law Review* 117, no. 6 (2004): 1765, 1766–67.

2 Snyder v. Phelps, 562 U.S. 461 (2011) ("[A]s a nation"); Sorrell v. IMS Health Inc., 131 S. Ct. 2653, 2670 (2011) ("Speech remains protected"); Hustler Magazine, Inc. v. Falwell, 485 U.S. 46, 55 (1988) ("may have an adverse"); Village of Skokie v. Nat'l Socialist Party of Am., 373 N.E.2d 21, 24 (Ill. 1978) ("We do not doubt").

3 Chaplinsky v. New Hampshire, 315 U.S. 568, 571–72 (1942); Rodney A. Smolla, "Words 'Which by Their Very Utterance Inflict Injury': The Evolving Treatment of Inherently Dangerous Speech in Free Speech Law and Theory," *Pepperdine Law Review* 36, no. 2 (2009): 317, 320–21.

4 See Brandenburg v. Ohio, 395 U.S. 444 (1969) (setting out current test for incitement); Thomas F. Shea, "'Don't Bother to Smile When You Call Me That'—Fighting Words and the First Amendment," *Kentucky Law Journal* 63 (1975): 1, 2, quoted in Shiffrin, *Dissent, Injustice, and the Meanings of America*, 74.

5 Smolla, "Words," 357.

6 Whitney v. California, 274 U.S. 357, 375 (1927) (Brandeis, J., concurring); Stanley Fish, *There's No Such Thing as Free Speech, and It's a Good Thing, Too* (New York: Oxford University Press, 1994), 109.

7 See, e.g., Milkovich v. Lorain Journal Co., 497 U.S. 1 (1990).

8 Jonathan Rauch, *Kindly Inquisitors: The New Attacks on Free Thought* (Chicago: University of Chicago Press, 2013), 166; Timothy C. Shiell, *Campus Hate Speech on Trial* (Lawrence: University Press of Kansas, 2009), 1. For a discussion of campus censorship, see Greg Lukianoff, *Unlearning Liberty: Campus Censorship and the End of American Debate* (New York: Encounter Books, 2013).

9 James Boyd White, *Living Speech: Resisting the Empire of Force* (Princeton, NJ: Princeton University Press, 2006), 41. See also Lee Bollinger, *The Tolerant Society* (New York: Oxford University Press, 1986), 12–13 (noting the disjunction between our personally held beliefs toward morally reprehensible speech and the legal protections for that speech).

10 Gay, Lesbian, and Straight Education Network, "The 2013 National School Climate Survey: The Experiences of Lesbian, Gay, Bisexual, and Transgender Youth in Our Nation's Schools" (2014), 12, 16, http://www.glsen.org/sites/default/files/2013%20National%20School%20Climate%20Survey%20Full%20Report_0.pdf; Nuxoll ex rel. Nuxoll v. Indian Prairie School Dist. #204, 523 F.3d 668, 672 (7th Cir. 2008) (upholding the right of a student to wear a shirt with the words "Be Happy Not Gay").

11 Jonathan Chait, "Not a Very P.C. Thing to Say: How the Language Police Are Perverting Liberalism," *New York Magazine*, January 27, 2015.

12 Kevin Cullen, "Gordon College Insults Our Intelligence," *Boston Globe*, July 15, 2014; Hemant Mehta, "Tufts University's Nondiscrimination Policy No Longer Applies to Religious Student Groups," *Patheos* (December 8, 2012).

13 The definition of "bigot" is taken from the online Merriam-Webster dictionary, available at www.merriam-webster.com. For similar arguments, see Steven D. Smith, "The Jurisprudence of Denigration," *U.C. Davis Law Review* 48 (2014): 675.

14 See also Richard W. Garnett, "Religious Freedom and the Nondiscrimination Norm," in *Matters of Faith: Religious Experience and Legal Response*, ed. Austin Sarat (New York: Cambridge University Press, 2014), 194, 197, 208; Patrick S. Shin, "Is There a Unitary Concept of Discrimination?," in *Philosophical Foundations of Discrimination Law*, ed. Deborah Hellman and Sophia Moreau (New York: Oxford University Press, 2013), 164.

15 Elizabeth Nolan Brown, "Women's College Cancels 'Vagina Monologues' Because It Excludes Women without Vaginas," *Hit and Run* (blog), January 15, 2015 (quoting a student characterizing the play as "blatantly transphobic"), http://reason.com/blog/2015/01/15/womens-college-cancels-vagina-monologues.

16 Erving Goffman, *Stigma: Notes on the Management of Spoiled Identity* (New York: Simon and Schuster, 1963), 3. See also Bruce G. Link and Jo C. Phelan, "Con-

ceptualizing Stigma," *Annual Review of Sociology* 27 (2001): 365, 370–71 ("When people are labeled, set apart, and linked to undesirable characteristics, a rationale is constructed for devaluing, rejecting, and excluding them").

17 Goffman, *Stigma*, 3, 5; Bollinger, *Tolerant Society*, 109–10.

18 White, *Living Speech*, xi, 32.

19 Susan J. Stabile, "Donald A. Gianella Memorial Lecture—What Is Religious 'Persecution' in a Pluralist Society?" *Villanova Law Review* 59 (2014): 753, 758.

CHAPTER 7

1 Burwell v. Hobby Lobby Stores, Inc., 134 S. Ct. 2751 (2014); Shadee Ashtari, "George Takei Blasts High Court's Birth Control Ruling, Calls for Hobby Lobby Boycott," *Huffington Post*, July 1, 2014.

2 Megan McArdle, "Hobby Lobby's Boycotters Aren't Crafty Enough," *BloombergView*, July 1, 2014; Rusty Pugh and Jenni Parker, "Decency Advocates Claim Victory as A&F Pulls Explicit Catalog, Ceases Publication," *American Family Association Online*, December 10, 2003.

3 Mark Berman, "How Apple, the NFL and Other Big Businesses Helped Kill the Arizona Bill," *Washington Post*, February 27, 2014; Lauren Raab and Kurtis Lee, "Backlash to Indiana Law Persists: NCAA, Others Welcome Change," *Los Angeles Times*, April 2, 2015.

4 Each of these forms of collective action can take place in physical or virtual spaces. See John D. Inazu, "Virtual Assembly," *Cornell Law Review* 98 (2013): 1093, 1100–1102.

5 The power imbalance does not always favor producers over consumers. See Lawrence A. Alexander and Maimon Schwarzschild, "Consumer Boycotts and Freedom of Association: A Comment on a Recently Proposed Theory," *San Diego Law Review* 22 (1985): 555, 558 ("Some (e.g., rich) consumers *qua* consumers have enormous leverage in a boycott whereas some producers *qua* producers do not").

6 Clayton Act, § 6, 38 Stat. 730 (1914) (current version at 15 U.S.C. §§ 12–27, 29 U.S.C. §§ 52–53 (2012)); National Labor Relations Act, 49 Stat. 449 (1935) (current version at 29 U.S.C. §§ 151-169 (2012)). I leave aside the question of public sector unions.

7 The assumption of a meaningful exit right is important and much debated. See, e.g., Oonagh Reitman, "On Exit," in *Minorities within Minorities: Equality, Rights and Diversity*, ed. Avigail Eisenberg and Jeff Spinner-Halev (New York: Cambridge University Press, 2005), 190.

8 N.A.A.C.P. v. Claiborne Hardware Co., 458 U.S. 886 (1982).

9 Ibid., 889, n. 26.

10 Brief for Petitioners, N.A.A.C.P v. Claiborne Hardware Co., 458 U.S. 886 (1982) (No. 81-202), 1982 WL 608671 ("Petitioner Brief"), *3, *31; *Claiborne Hardware*, 903–4.

11 *Claiborne Hardware*, 901–2.

12 Ibid., 902.

13 N.A.A.C.P. v. Claiborne Hardware Co., 393 So.2d 1290, 1301 (Miss. 1980); Claiborne County Co. v. N.A.A.C.P., Chancery Court of the First Judicial District of

Hinds County, Mississippi, No. 78,353 at 51b (August 9, 1976). The trial court also found that the boycott was an illegal secondary boycott.

14 *Claiborne Hardware*, 458 U.S. at 915.

15 Gary Minda, *Boycott in America: How Imagination and Ideology Shape the Legal Mind* (Carbondale: Southern Illinois University Press, 1999), 168.

16 Ross Douthat, "The Case of Brendan Eich," *New York Times*, April 8, 2014.

17 John Stuart Mill, *On Liberty*, ed. Edward Alexander (Toronto: Broadview Press, 1999), 74–75; Kirsten Powers, "Gay Marriage Debate's Sore Winners," *U.S.A Today*, April 7, 2015 (noting that Eich is still unemployed).

18 Conor Friedersdorf, "Mozilla's Gay-Marriage Litmus Test Violates Liberal Values," *The Atlantic*, April 4, 2014 ("no one had any reason to worry that Eich, a longtime executive at the company, would do anything that would negatively affect gay Mozilla employees"), http://www.theatlantic.com/politics/archive/2014/04/mozillas-gay-marriage-litmus-test-violates-liberal-values/360156/.

19 Ibid.; Andrew Sullivan, "Dissents of the Day," *Dish*, April 4, 2014, http://dish.andrewsullivan.com/2014/04/04/dissents-of-the-day-63/.

20 Douthat, "The Case of Brendan Eich."

21 Aaron Blake, "Anti-Gay Marriage Group Calls for Boycott of Mozilla Firefox," *Washington Post*, April 4, 2014; Gregg Keizer, "An Incredibly Shrinking Firefox Faces Endangered Species Status," *ComputerWorld*, March 5, 2015 (noting Mozilla Firefox's market decline), http://www.computerworld.com/article/2893514/an-incredibly rshrinking-firefox-faces-endangered-species-status.html.

22 Valerie Richardson, "New GoFundMe Rule Makes It Easy to Kill Christian Campaigns," *Washington Times*, April 30, 2015.

23 It is clear that some corporations like Mozilla and Hobby Lobby are highly expressive, but they are also highly regulated, and often viewed as closer to "the marketplace" than to "civil society." Whether the protections of the First Amendment or related statutes should extend to for-profit corporations has been highlighted in a number of recent cases. See, e.g., Citizens United v. Federal Election Commission, 558 U.S. 310 (2010); Burwell v. Hobby Lobby Stores, Inc., 134 S. Ct. 2751 (2014). See also Ronald J. Colombo, *The First Amendment and the Business Corporation* (New York: Oxford University Press, 2014).

24 Douthat, "The Case of Brendan Eich."

25 "Freedom to Marry, Freedom to Dissent: Why We Must Have Both," *Real Clear Politics*, April 22, 2014, http://www.realclearpolitics.com/articles/2014/04/22/freedom_to_marry_freedom_to_dissent_why_we_must_have_both_122376.html.

CHAPTER 8

1 Flynt, "My Friend, Jerry Falwell."

2 Robert D. Putnam, "*E Pluribus Unum*: Diversity and Community in the Twenty-first Century," *Scandinavian Political Studies* 30, no. 2 (2007): 141, 142, 148, 150–51. Putnam's thesis and methodology have been subjected to some challenges. See, e.g., Alejandro Portes and Erik Vickstrom, "Diversity, Social Capital, and Cohesion," *Annual Review of Sociology* 37 (2011): 461.

3 Putnam, "Diversity and Community," 164, 165.

4 John Danforth, *The Relevance of Religion: How Faithful People Can Change Poli-*

tics (New York: Random House, 2015), 46–47. The story of Wagner and Isaacson-Jones is also recounted in Tamar Lewin, "In Bitter Abortion Debate, Opponents Learn to Reach for Common Ground," *New York Times*, February 17, 1992.

5 Portions of this narrative draw from a video dialogue between Kevin Palau and Sam Adams. See Redeemer City to City, *Portland Case Study: Kevin Palau and Sam Adams* (2013), available at https://vimeo.com/66596545.

6 *Portland Case Study*; Samuel G. Freedman, "Help from Evangelicals (Without Evangelizing) Meets the Needs of an Oregon Public School," *New York Times*, August 9, 2013; Dan Harris, "Evangelicals Team with Portland's Gay Mayor for Charity," *ABC News*, December 25, 2011, http://abcnews.go.com/US/evangelicals-team-portlands-gay-mayor-charity/story?id=15218876.

7 Harris, "Evangelicals Team"; Freedman, "Help from Evangelicals"; *Portland Case Study*.

8 *Portland Case Study*; Jennifer Willis, "Finding Common Ground in Portland," *Faith and Leadership*, March 24, 2014. Romand Coles offers other examples of local political coalitions across difference in Romand Coles, *Beyond Gated Politics: Reflections for the Possibility of Democracy* (Minneapolis: University of Minnesota Press, 2005), 213–38 (discussing local organizing in the tradition of the Industrial Areas Foundation).

9 There are, of course, benefits to anonymity. For example, protecting one's identity can facilitate expression and communication that might otherwise be suppressed out of fear of stigmatization or retaliation. See NAACP v. Alabama, 357 U.S. 449 (1958) (holding that right of association protects disclosure of NAACP's membership list). But see Doe v. Reed, 561 U.S. 186 (2010) (holding that Washington citizens who signed an unsuccessful petition to overturn a state law recognizing same-sex marriage did not have a First Amendment right to remain anonymous).

10 Jim Dalrymple II, "How Ferguson's Rotting Suburbia Helped Create a Powder Keg," *Buzzfeed*, September 4, 2014.

11 Technology can also bridge our physical separation when we cannot be physically present with one another. My own sense is that face-to-face interaction is the best way to overcome physical distance. But we should not discount virtual alternatives that for some people will offer the only plausible means of interaction. The conservative homemaker in a rural Southern town may never have a face-to-face encounter with the progressive urbanite in Manhattan. But they may nevertheless share the possibility of online interaction. See John D. Inazu, "Virtual Assembly," *Cornell Law Review* 98 (2013): 1093, 1112–14.

12 Shane L. Windmeyer, "Dan and Me: My Coming Out as a Friend of Dan Cathy and Chick-fil-A," *Huffington Post*, January 28, 2013, http://www.huffingtonpost.com/shane-l-windmeyer/dan-cathy-chick-fil-a_b_2564379.html; Lesley Stahl, "Senator Tom Coburn: A Proud Contrarian," *60 Minutes*, December 21, 2014.

CONCLUSION

1 Some arguments for a different constitutional vision include Owen M. Fiss, *The Irony of Free Speech* (Cambridge, MA: Harvard University Press, 1996); Brettschneider, *When the State Speaks*; and Koppelman with Wolff, *A Right to Discriminate?*.

2 This last set of suggestions gestures toward an idea of federalism that also reinforces pluralistic and dissenting practices. See, e.g., Heather K. Gerken, "Dissenting by Deciding," *Stanford Law Review* 57 (2005): 1745, 1748 ("Disaggregated institutions create the opportunity for global minorities to constitute local majorities. They thus allow dissenters to decide, to act on behalf of the state"); Ernest A. Young, "The Rehnquist Court's Two Federalism," *Texas Law Review* 83 (2004): 1, 60–61 (suggesting that federalism serves as the "seedbeds of political competition," allowing nonmainstream views to develop at the local level).

3 The rise of online social activism brings many benefits, but not all of them translate into tangible action. See, e.g., Valeriya Safronova, "Millennials and the Age of Tumblr Activism," *New York Times*, December 19, 2014 ("[W]hether passion on Tumblr translates into participation in the real world is up for debate"); Molly Beutz Land, "Networked Activism," *Harvard Human Rights Journal* 22 (2009): 205, 205 ("Existing online advocacy efforts reveal a de facto inverse relationship between broad mobilization and deep participation").

4 Hill v. Colorado, 530 U.S. 703 (2000), and, 765 (Kennedy, J., dissenting).

5 McCullen v. Coakley, 134 S. Ct. 2518 (2014); Mass. Gen. Laws ch. 266, § 120E½(b).

6 Laurence Tribe, quoted in "Colloquium, Professor Michael W. McConnell's Response," *Pepperdine Law Review* 28 (2001): 747, 750.

7 Brief of the American Federation of Labor and Congress of Industrial Organizations as Amicus Curiae in Support of Petitioners at 1, *McCullen v. Coakley*, 134 S. Ct. 2518 (2014) (No. 12-1168).

8 Brief Amicus Curiae of the National Hispanic Christian Leadership Conference, et al., in Support of Petitioners, *McCullen v. Coakley*, 134 S. Ct. 2518 (2014) (No. 12-1168).

9 Laurence H. Tribe, "The Supreme Court Was Right to Allow Anti-Abortion Protests," *New York Times*, June 26, 2014.

10 Anne Blythe & John Frank, "Wearing Pink, Opponents of Abortion Restrictions Join 'Moral Monday' Effort," *News and Observer*, July 8, 2013 (noting that "Janet Colm, president and CEO of Planned Parenthood of Central North Carolina, was among the more than 60 arrested"); Anne Blythe, "Judge's Ruling to Dismiss 'Moral Monday' Cases Could Have Sweeping Effect," *Charlotte Observer*, August 3, 2014.

11 See Kenji Yoshino, "The New Equal Protection," *Harvard Law Review* 124 (2011): 47, 751 ("Pluralism anxiety flows from at least two sources—'new' kinds of people and 'newly visible' kinds of people").

12 W. Va. State Bd. of Educ. v. Barnette, 319 U. S. 624, 641 (1943).

13 George M. Marsden, *The Twilight of the American Enlightenment: The 1950s and the Crisis of Liberal Belief* (New York: Basic Books, 2014), 45; James Davison Hunter, *Before the Shooting Begins: Searching for Democracy in America's Culture War* (New York: The Free Press, 1994), 5, 9–10.

14 See also Sacks, *The Dignity of Difference*, 206 ("Optimism is the belief that things will get better. Hope is the faith that, together, we can make things better. Optimism is a passive virtue, hope is an active one. It takes no courage to be an optimist, but it takes a great deal of courage to have hope").

Index